LIVING WITH
WICKER

*Richard Saunders
and
Paula Olsson*

Photographs by Gary Denys

CROWN PUBLISHERS, INC., NEW YORK

Published by Crown Publishers, Inc.
201 East 50th Street, New York, New York 10022.
Member of the Crown Publishing Group.
CROWN is a trademark of Crown Publishers, Inc.
Manufactured in Japan

Library of Congress Cataloging-in-Publication Data

Living with wicker.
1. Wicker furniture—Collectors and collecting—United States.
NK2712.7.L58   1992
749.213′075—dc20   90-26730
ISBN 0-517-57184-6

10   9   8   7   6   5   4   3   2   1

FIRST EDITION

For Louise

CONTENTS

INTRODUCTION

Wicker furniture has recaptured the heart of America. Open any decorator magazine or interior design book today and you'll be showered with the unique visual freshness of wicker. The airy, three-dimensional quality of antique wicker was rediscovered and reevaluated some twenty years ago; the verdict then, as now, was "thumbs up!"

From the exotic handmade designs produced during the Victorian era to the austerity of the mission style and machine-made pieces of the twenties, wicker furniture has had a remarkable and most durable history. Since ancient times, wicker furniture has been constructed on the premise that woven furniture can "give" when in use, thereby creating an elasticlike flexibility that gently cradles the human body much like a basket. Outlasting tides of fashion because of its inherent adaptability, wicker was sometimes tailored to fit stylistic trends but never lost its identity.

Antique wicker has not only brought back a warm nostalgic aura into today's homes but also has added versatility, comfort, and a surprising vitality to modern interiors. Over the past two decades, interior decorators have relied on its individual and organic look to lighten rooms while at the same time adding a touch of romance. Once considered mere accent pieces, wicker furniture is found in every possible setting today and is as appropriate in elegant city apartments and suburban living rooms as around the hearth and on the verandas of country homes.

One of the most sought after items on today's antiques market, wicker furniture made between the end of the Civil War and the beginning of the Depression is enjoying an unprecedented renaissance. The old guard is finally giving wicker some long-overdue respect, no longer cavalierly brushing it off as mere "porch furniture." Museum curators are eagerly examining it like other forms of nineteenth- and early-twentieth-century furniture and making note of the manufacturer, date of production, rarity, and finish. Indeed, the decade of the 1990s is destined to be a time when serious attention is paid to wicker; the first major museum exhibition totally dedicated to antique wicker furniture is scheduled to take place in 1992 at the Renwick Gallery, part of the Smithsonian Institution in Washington.

It is our sincere hope that this book will open up minds as well as decorative possibilities. Artistic by design and eclectic by nature, wicker furniture is a perfect decorating medium. When combined with other furnishings, wicker magically creates a dreamlike atmosphere without mocking or competing with the more conventional pieces. Wicker adds an exotic mystique to any room, but never cries out for attention. It doesn't have to—it simply breaks old tired rules, complements a plethora of decorating motifs, and adds pizzazz to one's home and life.

LIVING
WITH
WICKER

WICKER: AN AMERICAN ORIGINAL

WICKER FURNITURE IS A TRUE American art form that has been ignored or, at best, grossly underrated for most of its 150-year history in this country. After collecting, restoring, researching, and writing about antique wicker for the past twenty years, we have come to accept one undeniable fact: the wicker furniture industry per se was born on American soil, and wicker is just now being recognized as one of the few forms of furniture developed in this country that did not rely heavily on existing European or Oriental styles. Born out of an improbable Horatio Alger–type rags-to-riches melodrama set in 1840s Boston, wicker furniture grew into a highly unconventional craft and ultimately evolved over the decades into the stylish woven wonders that are now eagerly sought by both antiques collectors and interior designers as classic examples of functional art. The finest wicker furniture ever made was produced by hand in America.

Lest you feel we're waving the Stars and Stripes to create a breeze, we will say at the outset that one of the goals of this book is to right some wrongs and clear up some long-held misconceptions about wicker furniture. While both the industry and the artful designs employed in the making of fine wicker pieces were born in the United States, the general public still has the impression that wicker furniture originated in the Far East. This is not true. The widespread confusion was undoubtedly nurtured by the fact that reed and cane, both of which are used in wicker manufacturing, are both derived from the rattan palm, a prolific vinelike plant that grows wild in the East Indies. Further adding to the mix-up is the abundance of poor-quality wicker reproductions from the Orient that have been imported into this country for the past thirty years. Loosely based on American Victorian wicker designs, these hastily produced "reproductions"—and we use the term loosely—have done immeasurable harm to the reputation of quality antique wicker. Over the years we've heard our share of complaints about how wicker is flimsy or rickety. After having a bad experience with an inexpensive reproduction, most people jump to the conclusion that all wicker is fragile, and therefore they avoid it altogether. However, after studying the genuine article and the reproductions, there is virtually no room for comparison. An imported piece of new wicker from the Far East may lend an airy touch to a room, but it will fall apart after a few years of use. Not unlike the flashy false front of a movie set, repro wicker is pure Hollywood—here today and gone tomorrow.

Quality antique American-made wicker is finally being taken seriously, and museums across the country are adding it to their collections. In 1986 New York City's Metropolitan Museum of Art celebrated the Aesthetic Movement, which introduced decorative arts into American goods in the 1800s, with a landmark three-month exhibition called "In Pursuit of Beauty." Antique wicker furniture was represented in this show and was given a good deal of scholarly attention.

From a stone sculpture from ancient Syria (circa 2600 B.C.) that depicts the steward Ebih-il on a round hassock of woven reed to the prestigious museum exhibitions of today, wicker furniture has not only spanned the centuries but, appropriately enough, has woven them

Although this 1880s Turkish bench is dripping with scrollwork, wooden beads, and curlicues, it is also a functional piece of furniture in a modern bathroom. Its versatility allows it to be moved in front of a dressing stand and used as a vanity bench, piled with plush bath towels, or used as a caddy for bath accessories.

together in a historical tapestry of amazingly intricate design. The craft of wickerwork furniture actually evolved from the longtime Egyptian tradition of basketry since 4000 B.C., using local palms, dried grasses, and swamp reed. The ancient Egyptians made some finely woven stools, coffins, cosmetic boxes, and chests, many examples of which were unearthed in 1922 when the fourteenth century B.C. tomb of King Tutankhamen was discovered. Early wicker furniture was also made in ancient Greece and China, in the Roman Empire, and in medieval England, where "basket chairs" were made of peeled willow twigs by basketmakers known as "twiggies." However, the one thing that all early wicker has in common is that it was considered a "people's furniture"—informally made by local craftsmen using materials that were readily at hand.

While the first piece of wicker furniture in the American colonies arrived, quite appropriately, on the *Mayflower* in 1620—it was a finely woven cradle used to rock baby Peregrine White to sleep—it was actually either made in Holland or imported there from China. Household records from seventeenth-century America tell us that crude, homemade wicker chairs from the British Empire and Europe were fairly common in this country. Nevertheless, it would take another 200 years before wicker furniture graduated from a humble craft into a bona fide industry.

It was on Boston's waterfront in 1844 that a young grocer named Cyrus Wakefield observed a large quantity of rattan being dumped on the docks after having served its purpose to secure cargo aboard a clipper ship on its return

voyage from the Far East. After examining one of the long, flexible poles, Wakefield decided that furniture could be made from this strange material and, with virtually no experience in this field, began experimenting by making numerous pieces of crude rattan furniture.

Within a few years Wakefield wisely quit the grocery business and decided to import whole rattan from China to meet the growing demand in America for split rattan, or cane—the glossy outer skin of the rattan vine, which was used for weaving chair seats. While building his business he continued to experiment not only with rattan but with reed—the inner pith of the rattan

The pre–French Revolution grandfather clock that dominates this living room is balanced by two natural Victorian wicker pieces. The side table has a unique reed and wooden ball motif along the legs; the three-tiered music stand is used here to display bric-à-brac.

∽

15

vine, which until that time had always been treated as waste. He soon found that reed was more pliable than rattan and began stepping up his furniture-making experiments by using this newly discovered material.

In the mid-1850s Cyrus Wakefield moved to South Reading, Massachusetts—later renamed Wakefield in his honor—where he quickly established the Wakefield Rattan Company, now the acknowledged granddaddy of the American wicker industry. An interesting point here: Wakefield chose to use the word "rattan" in his company title rather than "wicker" simply because before the turn of the century the latter term was infrequently used. Wicker furniture manufacturers of the pre-1900 era used the better-known terms "rattan" or "reed" to describe the furniture. Today, with hindsight, we can see that neither of these words accurately defines the type of furniture these firms were producing because rattan, reed (round or split), cane, and willow were more often than not combined in the making of a single piece. Wicker (from the Swedish *wika,* to bend, and *vikkerr,* meaning willow) is not a material in itself, but has evolved into an umbrella term that covers all woven furniture made from such materials as rattan, cane, reed, willow, Oriental sea grass, rush, fiber, raffia, and a host of various dried grasses.

Terminology aside, the Wakefield Rattan Company found its fair share of competition from the firm of Heywood Brothers and Company of Gardner, Massachusetts, from the 1870s to the late 1890s. The intense competition between the two rival manufacturers not only led to the refinement of existing styles but also encouraged experimen-

tation that culminated in an incredible explosion of flamboyant designs. This era is now known as the Golden Age of Wicker. All the stops were pulled out; creativity ruled the day. Wicker became the sweetheart of Victorian society.

Surprisingly, this all-out rivalry came to an abrupt halt in 1897 when the two titans of the industry decided to merge and formed the Heywood Brothers and Wakefield Company. It proved to be a consolidation that all but monopolized the wicker furniture industry from the turn of the century through the 1920s. During this period the newly formed company pooled the top line of craftsmen, designers, and business minds from both companies and came up with the cream of the crop in all three fields. One of Henry Heywood's first acts as president was to establish two new warehouses in London and Liverpool, thereby creating an export market and expanding the total number of warehouses to eleven. This, coupled with the fact that the new company had huge factories in Gardner and Wakefield, Massachusetts, as well as Chicago and San Francisco, discouraged serious competition.

There were many other firms making wicker items during these early decades, most notably the American Rattan Company of Fitchburg, Massachusetts; the Colt Willow Ware Works of Hartford, Connecticut; the Bielecky Brothers of New York City; the Chittenden-Eastman Company of Burlington, Iowa; the A. H. Ordway Company of South Framingham, Massachusetts; and the Paines Furniture Company of Boston. Nevertheless, to this day the names Heywood and Wakefield are linked with superiority in wicker design, workmanship, and materials.

This 1880s high-backed armchair with a hexagonal star-caning pattern woven into its backrest is a perfect balance for a cushioned banquette and painted table. An exotic blackamoor adds a capricious note to a relaxed dining nook.

∽

The fluid lines of natural Victorian wicker pieces create an interesting corner in a sewing room. The reception chair combines two unusual elements: an oval filigree backrest and a circular woven seat outlined with curlicues. The rare heart-shaped sewing basket has a closely woven hinged lid and woven reed gallery for additional sewing implements.

∽

A Victorian side table and armchair create a cheerful
mood on a sunlit Cape Cod landing. The fanciful aura is
enhanced by the nautical screen and folk art dog.

In this masculine bedroom with a nautical theme the 1920s three-drawer sideboard and 1890s platform rocker prove an attractive and functional mix. The chair's base is stationary; it rocks on steel rods to eliminate the carpet wear associated with conventional rockers.

A rolled-arm Victorian rocker with a circular star-caned back panel adds an exotic vitality to a Cape Cod living room. The wicker not only co-exists with the wonderful Hitchcock caned settee and early American rush-seated rocker, but they also complement each other in this warm and expansive atmosphere.

෨

This graceful rocker with rolled arms and a sym-metrical, crisscross reed backrest neutralizes the heavy Renaissance Re-vival walnut dresser to create an authentic Victo-rian bedroom setting. One of the decorative qualities of wicker is that a single piece can often balance an entire room of heavy wooden furniture.

෨

The graceful curves of a 1890s gentleman's rocker balance the straight lines and angles of the golden-oak wainscoting in the library of this beautiful Massachusetts Victorian home. Imaginative use of the stick-and-ball technique distinguishes the design. A Brunschwig & Fils fabric covers the seat cushion.

This late Victorian gentleman's armchair invites you to sit back and relax with a good book. The classic rolled-arm design is one of the most popular ever manufactured, having been a favorite of the public from the 1880s to 1910. The room's dark woodwork is complemented by the light-oak natural stain on the wicker.

White on white. A classic white wicker open-weave rocker gives a light lift to an already airy bathroom. Although it dates from around 1910, it neverthe-less has a strong Victorian influence. The corner shelf of turned wood has no actual reed or wickerwork but is reminiscent of many Victorian wicker designs.

~

The love of ornament was an acknowledged Victo-rian preoccupation. Here metal and reed prove the point: the massive yet ornately detailed iron and chrome-plated Radiant Acorn wood-burning stove and the delicate wicker lady's rocker and sewing basket (here doubling as a planter) are fine examples of this obsession from the late nineteenth century.

~

In the right setting white wicker lightens and brightens.
Here a darkly paneled sitting room is transformed by
a matching Victorian white table, rocker, and settee
that feature serpentine lines and wooden beadwork.
The fire screen and side table are also from the 1880s;
the floor lamp and tea cart are from the 1920s.
All the pieces interact to convert the room into
a harmonious and cheerful refuge.

This rolled-armed suite in the so-called horseshoe motif is a wicker collector's dream: a classic design with the original forest-green stain applied at the factory of the Heywood Brothers and Wakefield Company.

An 1890s settee and table add a decidedly nostalgic air to an otherwise contemporary living room. The closely woven Heywood Brothers and Wakefield Company settee employs an interesting center panel of open fancywork; the round table emphasizes rolled skirting, beadwork, curlicues, and graceful rolled cabriole legs.

Soft candlelight reflects the beauty of the warm, natural finish on these Heywood Brothers and Wakefield Company wicker pieces. The heart-shaped reception chair and ornate side table with cabriole legs and Turkish roll feet add to the digni-fied ambience of a Victo-rian-style music room.

∽

A bedroom is filled with 1890s wicker finished in the original golden-oak stain. The rare dressing stand, Turkish chair, and "fancy cabinet" (here used as a bookcase and curio shelf) create a functional vanity for the dressing area. Three examples of pictorial sailors' valentine shell collages in octagonal wooden frames and a rare miniature Victorian scrap screen restate the romanic theme of this charming room.

∽

25

After this Olympic-size pool was built in the Berkshires, it was enclosed by a barn transplanted from upstate New York. The fine lines of the informal wicker grouping
serve as a foil for the massive rustic beams overhead
and add lightness and dimension to the scene.

Classic rolled-arm gentleman's armchairs painted blue-gray enhance the cool colors of a turn-of-the-century California bungalow. Victorian antique toys and accessories add a fun-filled accent to the room and include an American rocking horse, a French horse race game, and a child-sized mannequin dressed in a custom-made uniform designed for a naval officer's son.

The Gothic lines of a handsome five-foot-tall étagère add an elegant touch to an otherwise spartan corner. The piece was custom made by the Wakefield Rattan Company for Boston's chief of police; the current owners have the original 1880 bill of sale.

∽

In this music room a Steinway grand piano is surrounded by rare music-related Victorian wicker. The four-tiered music stand at the left with an oval beveled mirror and the smaller music stand at the right were both made in the 1880s by the Wakefield Rattan Company. Behind the piano is a swivel piano chair and to its right is a music cabinet that includes a spacious storage area with a lyre motif on its door.

∽

Wicker and a playful array of children's toys bring comfort and a sense of whimsy to this entryway corner. The diamond designs in the weave of the 1920s forest-green armchair are painted a lighter hue to draw the eye to this pattern in an otherwise closely woven style. The floor lamp from the same era has an Eiffel Tower base and a graceful serpentine-shaped shade. A collection of toys and folk art are displayed on the stairs below a framed vintage July Fourth child's parade costume.

∽

29

THE AESTHETIC MOVEMENT

*T*HE ERA BETWEEN THE CIVIL WAR AND the end of World War I was an age of great transformation. The Aesthetic Movement, a period of tremendously rich and varied artistic activity in the United States in the last third of the nineteenth century, played an important role in the transformation of American life. Aestheticism took its cue from several Victorian reform movements whose aim was the regeneration of interior design and the arts. The use of the word "art" in relation to furniture or decoration became popular in America by the late 1870s and indicated an unfavorable reaction to mid-Victorian taste and to poorly designed products of the Industrial Revolution. The Aesthetic Movement emphasized individualism, singing the praises of handcrafted furniture rather than impersonal mass-produced products. A sense of lightness and a spirit of experimentation invaded late-Victorian homes; wicker furniture, with its airy weave and unusual designs, could not have come along at a better time.

Encouraging the imaginative use of materials, the Aesthetic philosophy meshed perfectly with the medium of wicker. "Art for art's sake" was the cry of the day. The Irish author Oscar Wilde became the movement's most ardent proponent during his famous American lecture tour of 1882 by speaking about the decorative arts and interior design in such a way that virtually every level of society fell under the spell of Aestheticism. This extraordinary period of creative appreciation by the masses led to the belief that an artistic interior would have a spiritually uplifting influence on its occupants.

Within the context of the Aesthetic Movement the cult of Orientalism also influenced Victorian wicker design. After Commodore Matthew Perry opened Japan to trade with the West in 1854, American consumers became increasingly fascinated with that Oriental country's unique tradition in the decorative arts. The Japanese displays at the London International Exhibition of 1862 and the wildly popular Japanese Bazaar at the 1876 Philadelphia Centennial Exhibition added to the fervor for anything exotic. Gradually American wicker manufacturers began employing the asymmetry of Oriental art, and these Anglo-Japanese designs captivated the public. The Japanese fan motif was delicately woven into the back panels of many an armchair and rocker of the period. Once again it's easy to see why some Victorian wicker designs are psychologically linked with the Orient.

Not only were the materials imported from the Far East but certain designs during this period were actually made to look as if they were imported from a faraway exotic land. It's ironic that all the wicker furniture designs that are considered to have been influenced by Orientalism were actually designed and handmade in the United States.

The novelty of Orientalism peaked in the 1880s and gave rise to a trend in interior design which relied heavily on Oriental art and exotica of all kinds. According to Russell Lynes in his book *The Tastemakers* (Dover Publications, 1980), this was the day of the cozy corner, the inglenook, the Oriental Booth:

In the corners of living rooms, not only of houses but of city apartments, housewives arranged curtains and sofas and cushions to make what were almost rooms within rooms. A few yards of striped material, a few curtain rods spiked with spearheads, a cot, and a batch of pillows were enough to make something an Arab could have called home.

The furniture of choice in these cozy corners was, of course, wicker. Oriental fabrics were often used as upholstery, and exotic accoutrements included peacock feathers, Persian carpets, blue-and-white china, fans, scrolls, ebonized hanging cabinets, colorful Japanese parasols, paper lanterns, mats, and hand-painted Japanese tiles. Cozy corners were secret hideaways, often made even more intimate by the use of screens that divided them from the rest of the room. "Screening" was a popular decorative device throughout the Victorian era. There were hand-painted and embroidered standing screens as well as folding screens of papier-mâché decorated with pressed flowers. The darling of the Aesthetic Movement, however, was the folding "scrap" screen. Usually constructed of two to four folding panels, these were lovingly created by the woman of the house. After purchasing a wood-framed screen with blank panels, she would proceed to painstakingly place cutout scraps of her favorite color illustrations, lithographs, and cards and then carefully paste them onto the panels and preserve her handiwork under a coat of clear varnish. Although there are precious few wicker folding screens from this era, there are many fireplace screens—small, single-panel designs produced specifically for decorative purposes to cover the hearth when not in use.

Mixing the romantic and the exotic was the essence of the Orientalism craze in America in the 1880s. Here the romantic is typified by the beguiling heart-shaped armchair and the exotic is represented by the eighteenth-century painted-silk Chinese mural and Oriental rugs.

The growing number of people involved in the Aesthetic Movement, fearing that mass-produced furniture would smother the creativity and artistic integrity of handmade furniture, began relying on advice from "tastemakers" who could guide their readers to make discriminating decisions in the field of interior decoration. Household advice books such as Charles Locke Eastlake's classic *Hints on Household Taste* (published in England in 1868 and in the United States in 1872), Clarence Cook's popular book *The House Beautiful* (1878), and the works of Andrew Jackson Downing were studied in earnest. Influential magazines of the period also greatly shaped the public's perception of the artful interiors, among them *Century Magazine*, *Harper's*, *The Ladies' Home Journal*, *Art and Decoration*, *Decorator and Furnisher*, *Good Furniture*, and *Architectural Record*. While wicker furniture was a recurring subject in many of these publications, it was Gervase Wheeler, author of the taste manual *Rural Homes*

This exquisite 1880 Anglo-Japanesque style sofa, manufactured by the Wakefield Rattan Company, was included in the landmark 1986 Metropolitan Museum of Art exhibition "In Pursuit of Beauty." The hand-crank wicker phonograph (at right), an extremely rare late-Victorian floor model, plays early cylinder records.

A *nineteenth-century papier-mâché reception chair with mother-of-pearl accents and gold-leaf detailing is complemented by a 1920s wicker cornucopia flower stand that serves as a towel holder. Miscellaneous accessories include a collection of Peking glass perfume bottles from the 1920s and a Staffordshire pirate figurine.*

∽

(1851), who first treated wicker in a serious manner when he wrote about the New York firm of J. & C. Berrian:

The principal excellencies of cane as a material for chairs, sofas, baskets, etc., etc., are its durability, elasticity, and great facility of being turned and twisted into an almost endless variety of shapes; hence in chairs there is every assistance given by it in obtaining that greatest of all luxuries—an easy seat and a springy back.

Wheeler went on to discuss the old-fashioned, heavy fire screens and the lighter but clumsy-looking basketwork used as a substitute, which he said had been superseded by articles made from cane, a material which though appearing slender and light, was actually tough and very strong. "Of light, fanciful, and ornamental things within the house," he proclaimed,

the infinite variety the material will permit precludes a description; for the library, a paper basket, for the boudoir, or ladies' room, a work-stand . . . for the drawing room, the ombra, or bay window, a flower stand, within which is a metal lining for holding water or wet sand. These are all substantial in construction, and by no means the fragile, easily broken articles they may look. . . .

Art furniture of all types demanded the attention of late nineteenth-century Americans. There was exotic-looking furniture made of bamboo as well as the inventive faux bamboo—actually turned bird's-eye maple which was "jointed" and stained to simulate the real thing. There was rustic furniture made from rough-hewn tree branches and roots in the Adirondack Mountains and used to furnish the summer retreats of the wealthy. Michael Thonet's graceful bentwood furniture was eye-catching and durable; cast-iron and twisted-wire furniture was popular in the garden; even papier-mâché furniture had its brief day in the sun. But wicker furniture was the crowning achievement of the Victorian era. Its very nature welcomed imaginative designs and innovative styles. It did not rely on one particular "revival" style but rather borrowed from an amazing array—including Gothic, French Rococo, Chinese, classical, Japanese, and Elizabethan—and ultimately created its own unique identity. The mixing of styles and the practice of combining four and five different materials in the making of a single piece ultimately led to the creation of a new functional art form which was wholeheartedly celebrated in its heyday and today has blossomed into a full-fledged wicker renaissance.

An unobstructed view of Point Lobos State Reserve on California's majestic central coast frames this sunlit bedroom corner. The wicker reception chair and curvaceous French iron hat rack create an open feeling and are contrasted with an English camelback pine trunk.

∽

Bright light streams in on white wicker in a sunny, fresh-looking dressing room. The divan —sometimes called a bustle bench, a piece often used as a prop in Victorian photography studios —has upholstery that was added by the current owner. The small 1920s stand at left is considered a side table while the Victorian piece at right is correctly termed a taboret because of its size and long skirting.

∽

A *collection of antique German bisque dolls is displayed in a bedroom with several children's wicker pieces from the Victorian era. The star-caned standing crib and doll's buggy carry these little ladies in style. The rare child's washstand, complete with towel racks on each side, holds an English porcelain Kate Greenaway washbowl.*

This luxurious bathroom includes a contemporary Italian marble sunken tub, French–etched glass windows, an antique rustic carved bear hall tree from the Black Forest, and two pieces of Victorian wicker furniture. The extremely ornate reception chair takes advantage of a wide spectrum of techniques, including scrollwork, birdcage designs along the posts and front legs, curlicues, and wooden beadwork. The ottoman at right doubles as a handy towel holder.

An intricately woven wicker florist's basket has its original gold paint and gesso roses. Antique French doors allow the sun to stream through painted glass panels into the bathroom. The custom-painted washbasin duplicates the swirling blue-ribbon design on the doors.

An elegant three-tiered Victorian wicker vanity has triple birdcage designs and cabriole legs which add a unique delicacy to a piece of this size. To the right a French painted chest accommodates a collection of nineteenth-century covered glove boxes.

Accessories to wicker furniture such as wood baskets, ferneries, and sewing baskets are often used to hold items not originally intended by their designers. An example is this Victorian music stand, now used as a book and magazine holder.

This very unusual Victorian plant stand looks more like an octopus than a piece of wicker. The exceptionally intricate braiding technique that silhouettes the piece is of special interest. The floor bricks are laid in a pattern resembling a Victorian crazy-quilt.

The rich hues of natural wicker add to the special ambience of this entryway. The Victorian workbasket has two maple shelves and is used here as a flower stand. The étagère of classic wicker design was included in the first joint catalog of the newly formed Heywood Brothers and Wakefield Company of 1898.

By the 1880s, "theme" pieces that highlighted common objects by having such designs as fans or musical instruments woven into their back-rests gained wide acceptance. This rocker displays a beguiling wedding bell motif and shares the spotlight with a side table and lady's armchair to create an artistic, sunny alcove. In the foreground a Roseville jardiniere adds contrast and color.

⌒

A rare Victorian piano chair with an adjustable swivel seat employs four elongated birdcage designs on the posts. The musical spirit of this corner is heightened by the antique pump organ, a folk art toy grand piano constructed from a crate, a small Schoenhut piano, a tin banjo, and a toy drum. Other toys include an early stenciled rocking horse and a late-Victorian lithographed Shakespearean theater complete with movable sets.

⌒

Two natural platform rockers made by the A. H. Ordway Chair Company of South Framingham, Massachusetts, complement rather than dominate this sunny breakfast room. An elaborate wire-and-wood birdcage sits atop a round table covered with an English lace tablecloth.

∾

A suite of 1890s wicker in a rare cattail design creates an atmosphere any cozy corner proponent of the Aesthetic Movement would find stimulating. A rocker, platform rocker, settee, umbrella stand, and side chair round out this remarkable set. The thicker cattail sections at the top of each piece were made by wrapping plied reed along the shafts. The overall theme is further reinforced by real cattails placed in the umbrella stand and a quilt wall hanging with a cattail-and-lily pattern.

∾

41

The design of this rich-looking gilded wicker divan from the 1890s creates a wavelike effect through the generous use of curlicues which virtually outline the piece. In the foreground a pair of French Art Nouveau rooster andirons holds a large antique chest. An Italian carved wood curio cabinet with mother-of-pearl decoration stands against the textured adobe walls.

An authentic re-creation of a Victorian parlor in a contemporary home captures the gracious splendor of a magical era. The rich color of the wallpaper and reefed curtains set the mood of the room. The Chittenden & Eastman black-painted wicker rocker and English horn chair are classic examples of Victorian excess in design.

This natural Victorian wicker grouping overlooks a
sunset off Long Island Sound. Four matching chairs
are placed around an exquisite square table. Of special
interest is the divan at the right which exhibits a flowing
leaf-shaped back and forest-green fancy-colored reeds.

A remodeled Cape Cod carriage house incorporates the
original horse stalls in the living room to add a touch of
country charm. The vertical iron bars act as a stark visual contrast to the fluid lines of the lightly stained
wicker settee and corner chair from the 1890s. The four-
panel Victorian English scrap screen adds dimension to
the room and serves as an intriguing backdrop.

Wicker furniture painted black can lend an air of elegance to any room. This reception chair from the 1880s is especially decorative with its butterfly motif of wooden beadwork and curlicues. To the left is an elaborate two-tiered French wire birdcage with a set-in clock.

ROMANCE IN THE AIR

BY THE LATE NINETEENTH century wicker furniture had become an essential element in the decoration of ''aesthetic'' homes. Inspired by the well-documented studio decor of the artists of the day, including James McNeill Whistler, Lawrence Alma-Tadema, Mary Cassatt, Robert Blum, and William Merritt Chase, the subliminal message was clear enough—wicker-inspired creativity. The public followed their lead without hesitation. While popular magazines carried illustrated articles about all of these artists as well as their studios, it seems that Whistler's workplace appealed to the ''artistic'' housewife more than the others. Whether this lopsided popularity stemmed from his genius of flamboyantly publicizing his works or was due to his dashing good looks is a matter for debate. As a signature on his paintings, Whistler used the butterfly, an image which, along with the sunflower, peacock, and lily, became solidly linked with the Aesthetic Movement. No wonder that during this era wicker manufacturers designed chairs with flaringly peacock-shaped backrests and sunflower motifs —they had fantasy value.

If the influential nineteenth-century writer William Kent was right in observing that "nature abhors straight lines," then nature must have loved Victorian wicker furniture. Consumers of the day seemed to feel that wicker could cast a romantic mood over an entire room, that its fluid serpentine lines and ornate detail would stimulate the imagination. There was a definite move away from dark musty rooms and toward lightness and freshness. What could brighten up a home with more style than the beguiling presence of wicker?

In the late nineteenth century a very special emphasis was placed on the concept of the home. A "real" home was expected to be an alluring sanctuary. In a rapidly changing and complicated world, the home was where Victorians found their greatest pleasures. It was an island of refuge, the interior of which was created for her family by the woman of the house. She not only became a sharp-eyed consumer of newly manufactured furniture and household items, but also took on the responsibility for turning out the handiwork that ensured the proper "homey" atmosphere.

Even the intricate and curvaceous lines of wicker furniture were not spared from fancywork. Chairs, rockers, and settees were further embellished with silk tassels, needlepoint cushions, crazy quilts, fringe, and even colorful satin ribbons lovingly woven

through the existing weaves. The Victorian housewife was not only encouraged to express her creativity in this way, she was expected to do so.

Ornate wicker of this period was thought to have an underlying sensuality that was a bit naughty for the times. Remember that Victorians were very much concerned with morality and respectability. While wicker was often visually linked with beautiful women in illustrations in romantic novels, magazine stories, and advertisements, it was also loosely associated with the forbidden world of the brothel. Respectable eroticism à la artist Lawrence Alma-Tadema's voluptuous nudes was acceptable, but photographs of nude prostitutes reclining on wicker chaise longues—most of them taken in the famous Storyville red-light district of New Orleans in the 1890s—were sinful. So, for a time, the exotic Far Eastern flavor of wicker furniture merged with its spicy, wickedly erotic aura.

Wicker became an acknowledged coquette of the Victorian era. There were settees backed by valentine hearts outlined by curlicues. There were tête-à-têtes—called "conversation chairs" in polite society—consisting of two joined chairs facing in opposite directions and designed to encourage the sharing of intimacies while limiting the temptation of physical contact by means of a dividing armrest. And there were divans, barely wide enough to accommodate two people, that were nevertheless intended for a friendly couple. For the vast majority of pre-1900 consumers, wicker furniture simply opened the doors to a variety of possibilities; it could be a place to sit or could be a flirtatious, saucy, even erotic piece of art. It depended entirely on one's frame of mind.

An 1880s natural settee with a double-heart motif backrest adds a distinctly romantic ambience to a relaxing garden room. The blue Oriental ceramic jardiniere and carved nineteenth-century rosewood garden seat in the foreground add an intriguing touch of exoticism.

A high-backed wicker conversation chair produces a courtly setting in an artistic corner of a Cape Cod cottage. This particular design was the finest of three offered in the first joint trade catalog of the Heywood Brothers and Wakefield Company of 1898. The curvaceous two-tone blue table lamp was made in 1915.

This magnificent living room grouping of natural Victorian wicker proves that not all so-called natural pieces were finished in the same manner. The decorative fire screen with an oval tapestry insert is stained a muted green, the leather cameo-backed rocker a golden oak, and the fabulous seven-foot-tall étagère and round table a rich mahogany. French Majolica, Belleek, and Royal Worcester china on the étagère add appealing accents.

This natural wicker platform rocker from the 1870s is a vision of Victoriana. Placed on a whitewashed plank floor in a kitchen alcove, the lines of this enduring design give a welcoming feel to a spacious contemporary home.

51

A *candlelit bedroom corner exudes Victorian roman-
ticism. The 1920s wicker vanity mixes well with the
voluptuous curves of the lady's armchair and ottoman.
The skirted side table in the background is topped
with a Battenberg lace tablecloth.*

This Victorian "sociable" was intended for an intimate couple to share. The closely woven design makes use of scalloped fancywork woven into both backrests and the skirting. The seat lifts up for storage. The ottoman, from the same era, also employs the scalloped-reed technique as well as wooden beadwork. The 1920s table lamp casts a discreetly subdued glow over the room.

The summery feeling of this room was created by the whimsical wall treatment of hand-painted ferns and latticework by Michel Poulion of Dorchester, Massachusetts. The airy setting is further enhanced by a Victorian wicker taboret with a hexagonal top and a fancy turn-of-the-century rocker.

The fluid lines of this late Victorian rocker and reception chair soften the angularity of the sunroom windows overlooking the blue sea off Nantucket, Massachusetts.

Wicker need not dominate a room to have a significant effect. This wicker table lamp with a unique vase insert below the shade is both functional and artistic. The multipaned windows are outlined with flowing hand-painted rose arbors by Michel Poulion of Dorchester, Massachusetts.

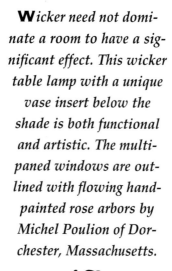

Catching the last of the afternoon sun through slightly parted lace curtains, the dreamy tranquility of this Massachusetts parlor cannot be denied. The Victorians' love of the sea is echoed in the 1890s shell-back settee. A rolled-arm gentleman's armchair from the same period is in the foreground; to the right an early Victorian needle-point armchair balances the grouping. The antique Persian Mahal rug adds warmth and a touch of the exotic.

The opulent detail work exhibited in this 1890s rocker is a testament to Victorian hand craftsmanship. By contrast, the four-tiered whatnot is uncommonly simple in design for a Victorian piece, embellished only by elongated birdcage designs between each shelf and a circular plied-reed finial.

∽

If well placed, even a single piece of wicker can add pizzazz to a room. Here a Victorian Turkish bench brings lyric style and intricate detail into a bedroom corner. Adding to the atmosphere, a classic marble bust sits atop a painted Arts and Crafts plant stand.

∽

The white wicker "comfort rocker" manufactured by the Larkin Chair Company of Buffalo, New York, and the side table behind it both date from the late 1890s and bring a touch of crisp vitality to this Massachusetts bedroom. The wicker softens the boldness of the English pine chest of drawers and the antique iron bed frame. The pitcher and bowl set on the side table is English Ironstone in the Florentine pattern.

A massive Eastlake double bed made of walnut and rosewood is a perfect foil for the fine lines of antique wicker. Here an 1880s oak-topped side table, a 1920s lamp, and a late Victorian platform rocker create a distinctly romantic corner.

Ideally a breakfast room should be not only a comfortable place in which to eat but also an informal sitting room. Here a late Victorian tilt-top table with Turkish-roll feet visually anchors the room, while a matching rocker and armchair from the same era create a balance. A 1915 tea cart in the foreground has a removable tray for convenient serving. At right a striking Weller plant pedestal and jardiniere and an Ushak Turkish carpet bring color into the room.

The abundance of wicker pieces on this Victorian sun porch are underplayed by the many accessories added to create a comfortable and inviting nook. The upholstered settee and table to its left are from the turn of the century; the table at right and the armchair are from the 1920s. The antique Sheffield silver tray sits on a contemporary custom-made hand-carved mahogany base.

While the American Victorian cottage set consisting of a double bed and commode is the center of attention in this bedroom, one's eye soon drifts toward the airy 1880s heart-backed rocker to the right. A Bar Harbor–style child's chaise longue at the foot of the bed also adds a whimsical touch.

∽

A dark floor and walls contrast with flowery fabric and white wicker to create a romantic feeling. This bedroom is dominated by the rare 1910 double bed made by James McCreery & Company of New York and sold by Lord & Taylor. The bed is flanked by two table lamps from the 1920s, each on a Victorian wicker side table.

∽

This set of wicker twin beds from the late 1920s was originally from Ernest Hemingway's Key West estate and is now in a private collection. An extremely ornate pair of matching Turkish benches are placed one at the foot of each bed; a wicker lamp sits on a Victorian serving table, here used as a bedside stand. The white wicker vanity (below) is in the same bedroom and is dramatically set off against the boldness of a dark flowered chintz drapery. The piece itself is from the 1920s and features a three-way beveled mirror and two drawers. A Bakelite dresser set from the same era adorns the top.

This rolled-arm beaded wicker chair was painted a pale peach tone to pick up the rich colors of the drapery and hand-loomed Irish carpet. The plush Aubusson tapestry headboard is enhanced by high whitewashed valuted ceilings. A French recamier at the foot of the bed and a mechanical singing bird in a gilded cage complete the poetic vision of Victoriana.

∽

The bedroom of this sunny Cape Cod summer house is accented by two Victorian wicker pieces. The fancy reception chair in the background lends grace to the angular corner by emphasizing the flowing nature of scroll-work; the rolled-edge ottoman at the foot of the bed is a handy slipper stool. Whimsical mermaids in three Ralph Cahoon paintings watch over the scene.

∽

An upholstered chaise longue covered in a flowery chintz fabric forms the centerpiece of this guest room corner. The restful setting is enhanced by a four-tiered wicker bric-à-brac stand and a serpentine armchair from the late Victorian era. The sisal matting floor is cool, practical, and a great complement to wicker furniture.

The subtly exotic blue-and-white bamboo print on the drapery and coverlets in this bedroom is an inspired match for the white wicker twin beds. Made in the 1920s by McCreery & Company of New York, the beds have the popular Art Deco diamond design woven into the head and footboards. The handsome table lamp was made during the same decade by the Heywood-Wakefield Company.

ﾌ

THE WINDS OF CHANGE

*A*ROUND THE TURN
of the century, a virtual revolution in wicker design began to spread across the country. A major shift in taste away from Victorian designs took hold seemingly overnight, and within a few years pieces with flowing lines or ornate detail work were being routinely rejected by the public. Although this reform movement was making its mark on other types of furniture as well, wicker was the most dramatically altered because it was so lavishly intricate in design. It also became one of the most visible targets of reform-minded tastemakers. These Americans had belatedly joined the ranks of the English Arts and Crafts Movement, which had its roots in the works of John Ruskin and William Morris. Under their influence, Victorian-style wicker, now an embarrassment to its owners, was

The original and unrestored paint and upholstery on a campy 1920s Lloyd Loom Turkish bench creates a unique visual contrast to the black-and-white tiles in a contemporary bathroom.

∽

abruptly exiled to the attic or carted to the junkyard. Wicker designs of the early 1900s that exhibited even a hint of Victorian elegance were laughed off showroom floors. Sales dropped off at an alarming rate. It was a perplexing dilemma for an entire industry that only yesterday had been thriving. American wicker manufacturers began asking themselves if it was possible that their product had passed its peak in popularity and was now plunging headlong into oblivion.

Ironically, it was not until Austrian, German, and English wicker imports of this transitional period began flooding the U.S. market with tremendous success that the American wicker industry was forced to face reality. Times had indeed changed, and the public had moved toward austerity by selecting European designs that were surprisingly conservative and angular in line. For the first time since Cyrus Wakefield began experimenting with rattan in the 1840s, American consumers were buying wicker furniture made outside their own country. Fortunately, it only took a few years for American manufacturers to adapt their wicker designs to the new style. The man who led the way was none other than Gustav Stickley.

Well known for his Craftsman (commonly called Mission) furniture made out of white oak, Stickley began making functional, straight-lined wicker furniture using peeled willow in the early 1900s. After traveling to England and the Continent in 1898, he returned to his company in Eastwood, New York, deeply influenced by the Arts and Crafts Movement, and adapted its principles to fit his own furniture designs. His massive, masculine-looking willow versions of his famous oak pieces boldly

restated his rejection of all that was Victorian. Although his closely woven willow furniture was recommended to break up the monotony of his Mission-style oak pieces, both fell under the edicts put forward in the introduction to his Craftsman Furniture catalog of 1910: "Anybody who knows Craftsman furniture," Stickley announced, "has no difficulty in perceiving that the principles upon which it is based are honesty and simplicity." He went on to explain that

when I first began to make it I did so because I felt that the badly-constructed, over-ornate meaningless furniture that was turned out in such quantities by the factories was not only bad in itself, but that its presence in the homes of the people was an influence that led directly away from the sound qualities which make an honest man and a good citizen. It seemed to me that we were getting to be a thoughtless, extravagant people, fond of show and careless of real value. . . .

One way to counteract this national tendency, he proposed, was to "bring about, if possible, a different standard of what was desirable in our homes."

Stickley's trade catalogs, produced between 1901 and 1913, and his popular service magazine, *The Craftsman*, not only showcased his furniture but imparted his philosophy of simplicity and sturdiness in home furnishings. The public loved Mission-style wicker, and due to the inherent adaptability of the form, other manufacturers were quick to realize that it was the wave of the future. By 1905 the Heywood Brothers and Wakefield Company and dozens of other wicker firms were producing huge quantities of Mission-style wicker to meet the public's demand while drastically cutting down on the number of

The austere atmosphere of this Stickley-inspired entryway is a study in Mission design. The two-tone willow armchair with blue-stained high-lighted edges, grandfather clock, and library table are all authentic Crafts-man pieces made by Gustav Stickley.

∽

designs employing the slightest degree of ornateness.

In 1910 a writer for *The House Beautiful* magazine summed up the prevailing public opinion when she wrote:

The improvement in design was everywhere noted; the absence of fancy effects, of whirli-gig rosettes and elaborate braiding which makers of wicker furniture, particularly those who worked in rattan, once thought the American public wanted. Good lines and good color combinations were the rule, and the exceptions were few and hard to find.

By 1910, Mission-style wicker was sharing the spotlight with a rounded and slightly more graceful design that relied on open latticework. It was called Bar Harbor. Although originally intended to serve as an alternative to the confining, boxlike lines dictated by the Mission style, Bar Harbor wicker quickly replaced its predecessor. Here was a simple approach that also capitalized on the airy three-dimensional quality of wicker by emphasizing crisscross reed openwork in the backrest, under the arms, and throughout the skirting. Manufacturers were overjoyed because this new design not only resulted in faster production time but also required far less materials than the closely woven Mission style. The public fell hard for Bar Harbor wicker—named after the famous seaside town in Maine—and it garnered a loyal following for the next twenty years. It seemed carefree and informal when compared to the strict conservative lines of Mission pieces. But most of all, it was extremely comfortable—a point not overlooked by a writer for *American Homes and Gardens* magazine in 1914. "The comfort of this kind of furniture," the reporter stated,

The lightly finished 1920s handwoven fiber armchair creates a relaxing atmosphere for this home in Potomac, Maryland. The floor lamp with a diamond-patterned shade and scalloped rim is also fiber.

largely depends upon the construction proportion used by the first designer. It also depends upon the style and shape of the arms whether or not one can really feel at ease in chairs one at times believes to have been made from fantastic designs emanating from the brain of a designer who was more intent on producing something new and original in chairs than making really comfortable seats for the poor mortals who are to sit on them. . . .

At the outbreak of World War I in 1914, economic conditions determined the type of wicker furniture on the American market. Due to the war a tremendous increase in import duties on rattan was put into effect, and wicker manufacturers were once again faced with an industry-threatening dilemma. The only alternative was to use different materials. The first effort was an unsuccessful attempt by the Department of Agriculture to create a domestic willow-raising industry. Then manufacturers turned to a product called ''fiber'' which had been little used but had been around since 1904. A strong but highly pliable twisted paper, fiber was a chemically treated synthetic material that bore a striking resemblance to reed and willow, especially when painted. Made to match the thickness of thin-gauge reed, fiber was sometimes wrapped around an inner core of wire to ensure strength and durability. Use of fiber—often called ''fiber reed''—made it feasible for manufacturers to produce closely woven designs because the material was so inexpensive.

Then, in 1917, a revolutionary machine was invented that would change the wicker industry forever—and ultimately play a major role in its demise. Marshall B. Lloyd, a maker of wicker baby carriages in Menominee, Michigan, perfected an ingenious device that wove spaghetti-thin strands of fiber in an over-and-under manner to form flat ''sheets'' of wickerwork. These woven sections could then be transferred directly from Lloyd's patented loom and fitted over preassembled frames. The Lloyd Loom was a sensation, doing the work of thirty men while at the same time cutting the cost to the consumer. The difference in price between Lloyd products and the hand-woven reed designs of the same era was substantial. Finally, after witnessing a healthy surge in sales over four consecutive years, the Lloyd Manufacturing Company was made a wholly owned subsidiary of the Heywood-Wakefield Company in 1921.

''**T**here is a danger in being too conservative,'' wrote Walter Dryer in a 1917 article in *The Art World* magazine.

There is no fundamental reason why the new should necessarily be bad, though it often is, and those of us who yield too far to reactionary tendencies may find that we have, in our ultra-conservatism, rejected something worth while, something which marks a real advance in mobiliary art.

The true criterion by which to judge a novelty, he continued, was whether it served some useful or decorative purpose more successfully than what had gone before. "Of all the furniture introductions of the past twenty years," he concluded, "I am inclined to think that wicker most completely meets that test."

This "ultra-conservatism" was, of course, a result of the overreaction against Victorian wicker. In 1925, the Paris exposition Internationale des Arts Décoratifs ushered in Art Deco–style wicker based on geometric lines, rational construction, and simple ornamentation. Art Deco pieces were most often handmade. The Lloyd Loom, with all its efficiency from a business standpoint, was incapable of producing anything but a simple wicker fabric, and by the middle to late 1920s many customers wanted something with more style. Pieces made in the Art Deco vein strove for harmony and proportion. Balance of design was of prime importance, and the now-familiar diamond pattern woven into the backs of chairs and settees restated the reliance on controlled geometric designs.

While the 1920s were dominated by inexpensive machine-made wicker, there were notable hand-woven examples which became classics in the field. The basic Bar Harbor design was improved upon by inserting drink receptacles and even handy magazine holders into chair arms for lazy readers. Electric table and floor lamps, available in a great variety of styles, were also big sellers. But on the whole, wicker was in a slump. By the late 1920s manufacturers were beginning to panic and tried a variety of styles including "stick wicker," which overemphasized vertical lines by using thick reeds widely spaced apart in groups of two. Yet nothing seemed to work, and when Old Man Depression snuck in the back door, it was the end of wicker's reign.

A unique and once flourishing industry had apparently lost touch with its roots. The strongest tie between wicker furniture and the public had always been the fact that it was handmade from natural materials. When the machine age entered the picture along with the Lloyd Loom and man-made fiber, the true art of wicker furniture was irretrievably lost.

Dark-blue staining highlights the streamlined Art Deco lines of a wide-armed natural wicker chair from the late 1920s.

ϖ

A *1920s wicker table lamp sheds light on a two-drawer wicker serving table from the same era. The top was hand-painted by artist Betsy Kolpecnick. The quilted runner with a single plate and long-stemmed rose to one side gives a trompe l'oeil effect and adds undeniable style to this all-white piece of wicker.*

&

This shingled porch on Nantucket was enclosed to create a sunny family room. The stylish willow desk and chair were made in 1915 by the Heywood Brothers and Wakefield Company.

∽

This Stickley-designed summer house includes a Mission-style oak dining set and buffet and a Mission-era art glass light fixture. The flared sides of the wicker plant stand under the draped window display its original two-tone paint job and add dimension and a touch of lightness to the room. Majolica accent pieces are artfully displayed on the wall and buffet to add a splash of color to the informal dining room.

✍

In a stylishly eccentric living room, a natural 1920s Perfek'tone wicker phonograph, manufactured by the Heywood-Wakefield Company, stands next to an early nineteenth-century Verguenza Spanish chest. On the wall is a painting of Viscount Wimbleton, knighted by Queen Elizabeth I in 1601, and his page. The bird's-eye view is from a bedroom loft.

✍

A *suite of Mission-style wicker furniture exemplifies the purity of form and simplicity of line cherished by followers of the Mission doctrine. The entire suite has its original forest-green paint and matching upholstery. The coffee table and window box are rarities in wicker design.*

A *late-1920s telephone table is now used as a desk in a young girl's bedroom. The pink-and-mauve color scheme adds a distinctively feminine touch.*

The off-white shingle treatment on an interior wall of a family room serves as a pleasing backdrop for wicker pieces. The 1920s wingback rocker, matching armchair, and two round side tables dating from the same era add to the relaxed simplicity of the room.

The color scheme of this reading corner creates a restful setting. The matching pair of armchairs, circa 1915, are unique to the era in that their closely woven wingback design is curved inward to create a sculptured effect. The round table, from the same period, is made of fiber.

Time flies in this cheerful corner which makes good use of brightly painted white wicker. The armchair, round side table, and upholstered Bar Harbor willow chaise longue were all made around 1915. The pineapple feet on the chaise longue were done with plied reed, a popular manufacturing technique of the era.

This set of stick wicker is a good example of the last collectible style of wicker furniture. The two-ply style became modestly popular in the mid-1920s and lasted into the 1930s. Stick wicker was handmade, but its stark vertical lines failed to capture widespread public acceptance. Today it is more popular than it was originally.

The rich wainscoting in the office of the Charlotte Inn on Martha's Vineyard makes a perfect backdrop for wicker picnic baskets and Model T automobile storage trunks from the 1920s.

A partially paneled den is a perfect background for wicker stained in earth tones. The flamboyant four-piece Art Nouveau "peacock" suite was handmade of fiber in 1910 by the Merikord Company of Sheboygan, Wisconsin. The original green-rubbed stain finish is augmented by gold highlights at distinct points in the design. The natural Victorian wicker two-panel screen, made by the Wakefield Rattan Company, serves as an interesting backdrop in this inviting room.

∾

A natural 1920s willow and Oriental sea grass rocker blends in perfect harmony with the white-washed pine treatment in this den. Inside the cushion-filled banquette, an 18th-century Dutch painting hangs on the back wall while a pair of nineteenth-century Gothic rain gutters used as sconces adorn the side walls.

∾

Wicker furniture for the bedroom is something most people do not consider, but here the natural 1920s double bed and mirrored chest are both attractive and functional. The antique quilt features the Tree of Life pattern.

Upholstered in a colorful Pierre Deux fabric, this side chair was handmade of reed around 1915. The durable sisal matting floor covering is actually a cousin to woven brush mats from the Victorian era, which were made by spinning the shavings from rattan into a yarn.

This striking bedroom is composed of a 1910 double bed, round side table, writing desk, and two wicker oil lamps from the early 1900s that have been converted to electricity. The quilt hung on the wall and the navy blue and white quilt on the bed add color and line.

*This magical wicker sun
room is filled with pieces
from the 1920s: an uphol-
stered settee and matching
armchairs, a tea cart, and
a small dining set. The
floor-to-ceiling windows
transform the room into a
brilliant sun space, mak-
ing it a favorite spot for
dining and relaxing.*

*This family room is filled with dark-stained fiber furni-
ture brightened with floral chintz to create a pleasing
contrast. The cluster of antique wicker trays, mounted
on a wall and used as sun catchers, proves the versatility
of wicker accessories. Directly below the trays a reverse
six-panel Aladdin lamp casts a warm glow over the
room. The sideboard and hutch are English pine.*

A *matching settee and armchair from 1910 both employ the popular three-ply round reed crisscross pattern set into the back-rests. The upholstered innerspring seats are covered with the same floral pattern found on the base of the glass-topped coffee table. The geometric lines of the wicker effectively soften the interior of this inviting living room at the Thorncroft Inn on Martha's Vineyard.*
∽

The distinctively mascu-line tone of the billiard room in this summer house in the Berkshires is both virile and artful. The antique bil-liard table, made by Charles E. Reich of Hart-ford, Connecticut, shares the spotlight with the col-ored-glass double doors and the hanging Mission-style Stickley light fixture. The understated 1920s dark-green wicker arm-chair in the corner serves as an inviting respite.*
∽

This handsome natural wicker suite from 1915 includes
a couch, rocker, and armchair with handy magazine
pocket and circular drink holder built into the arms.
An Eiffel Tower–style floor lamp and an unusual 1920s
sea grass armchair and matching ottoman, both with
lift-top seats for storage of sewing supplies, are in the
background. An old wooden chicken carrier with an
added glass top is used as a coffee table.

The bold, uncompromising look of darkly painted
wicker pieces creates a dramatic visual contrast against
the lightness of expansive French windows. The color
combination of black (the three-piece Lloyd Loom suite)
and teal (the turn-of-the-century table and fernery)
strikes a perfect balance. The natural table lamp from
the early 1920s adds to the carefully orchestrated
spectrum of colors in this sun room.

The oak stain on this natural wicker dining set is an attractive match for the cabinets and antique oak icebox in a country kitchen. The set was made around 1910 by the Heywood Brothers and Wakefield Company. The Mission-style wall clock and the turn-of-the-century caramel-glass hanging light fixture add interest.

A *variety of wicker styles are successfully combined in this sitting room. Each possesses a unique feature: the desk has a closely woven hooded top; the desk chair employs a reed back and all-wood bottom; the ottoman, used as a table, combines eccentric angular lines with curlicues; and the 1920s armchair has an unusual cameo-shaped caned back panel.*

౿

This gem of a platform rocker is both a treasure for the wicker connoisseur and a toy collector's dream. A rare salesman's sample from the late nineteenth century, it is slightly larger in scale than the bentwood chair to the right which was intended as a child's toy. Other antique toys include a folk art wooden ark, a tin German ocean liner, and a swinging acrobatic clown.

*H*AVING STEPPED
back into fashion over the past two decades, fine wicker furniture is now poised for flight to a far higher level of popularity
than ever before. Pre-1930 wicker is doubly attractive to today's buyers. It has not only reclaimed its hard-earned reputation as a unique decorative element in the home, but has also
become a wise investment in the antiques world.

While an 1881 article in *Scribner's* magazine described wicker
as "capital stuff to fill up the gaps in the furnishing of a country
house for the summer," today's eclectic style of decorating
encourages the use of wicker to create a unique blend of infor-
mality and dimension in any room in the home. Decorators
and collectors alike are once again creating entire rooms of old
wicker furniture—be it bedrooms, sun rooms, dining rooms,

or living rooms—and the results are at the same time whimsical and practical, exotic and inviting. Highly touted in the past as the perfect accent for any room in the house, individual wicker pieces that are carefully chosen and placed with care can still add charm and warmth to any interior.

Antique wicker has become the chameleon of home furnishings. That subtle quality called "atmosphere" is still on the mind of wicker consumers, and the correct combinations of design, finish, material, and pattern are of the utmost importance. Wicker can possess an aura of Victorian elegance or conjure up memories of lazy summer days on a shady porch. Simply put, wicker creates a mood.

During the Victorian era the great majority of wicker pieces were left "natural," that is, unpainted and either sealed with a clear varnish at the factory or stained and then varnished. Popular stains of the day included mahogany, walnut, forest green, cherry, oak, and ebony. While stains gave wicker a more finished look and were selected to complement specific color schemes in the home, the novel concept of "color work" was also widely practiced during the 1880s and 1890s. The purpose of this technique, called "fancy colored reeds" in advertisements and trade catalogs, was to draw attention to particularly intricate or graceful reedwork in the design by predyeing or painting individual reeds before weaving them into the piece. Muted green, pale red, ivory, and gold were the colors most often used, while the main body of the piece was left natural. The most impressive examples of this method were done in dark-green detail work which was woven into pieces employing a light walnut stain. When graceful organic designs resembling oak leaves, ferns, and willow trees were augmented by the subtle earth tones of green and brown, the results were at once calming and lyrical.

When writing about his Mission-style wicker furniture in 1915, Gustav Stickley assured readers of his *Craftsman* magazine that "willow furniture can be used in connection with almost any other kind of furniture and is an important item when a certain color scheme is to be carried out in a room because it will take a stain of any tone." While Stickley's willow pieces were usually finished with a clear varnish, a soft green stain, or a deep golden-brown stain, he would also take on customized

Wicker at its eclectic best: a Victorian armchair, graceful 1920s table lamp, oblong table, and angular turn-of-the-century pedestal plant stand combine to set the mood for an enchanting supper in this intimate dining room.

coloring, and was known to have stained his willow pieces various shades of blue and gray.

By the mid-1880s a limited number of wicker buyers began experimenting with painting their pieces to complement a specific decor. This was by no means a common practice at that time. But as a desire for sunlight, the increasing popularity of indoor plants—resulting in a marked increase in the use of wicker ferneries—and a trend to lighten up interiors in general swept the country, it should have been no great surprise when artistic-minded homeowners began painting their wicker furniture green, brown, black, white, and even gold. After all, this was the Gilded Age that Mark Twain wrote about in his novel of the same name. Painting highly ornate wicker gold was adding unnecessary ornamentation to something beautiful in its own right—but that's why it's called gilding the lily.

By 1910 a fascinating new painting technique called "Duo-Tone Enamel Finish" emerged as a favorite with the public. In August 1912 a writer for *American Homes and Gardens* magazine reported on this process after seeing a showroom with factory-painted wicker pieces finished in this interesting "antiqued" manner. "The painting of the furniture is so cleverly done that it is an art in itself," the article said.

Two or more tones of the same color are usually employed. The paint is thinned and the furniture treated to two coats of the lighter color. When this is dry, a coat of the darker color is brushed over, and when nearly dry, it is wiped off with a cloth. This allows the lighter color to show through while the darker color forms deep shadows in the crevices.

The resulting highlights, the reporter found, were "much more beautiful than when only one color is used. Paint that has a dull, flat surface when dry is best for this purpose," the article concluded.

By the 1920s, brighter factory-painted wicker in colors such as canary yellow, ming blue, jade, and turquoise was being offered to the public. The practice of painting the diamond-shaped design woven into the backs of many Art Deco pieces for dramatic accent was also at its zenith.

While a very limited number of Victorian wicker designs were upholstered at the factory—most notably the ever-popular and now rare Morris chairs—specific pieces such as cane-bottomed

An upstairs landing makes use of a striking wicker dining set from two distinct eras. Four matching rolled armchairs from the 1890s and a 1915 round dining table make a sophisticated blend that works well in this restored carriage house.

∽

reclining couches and chaise longues screamed for homemade cushioned comfort. The big push toward upholstered wicker actually came from German and Austrian designs from the turn of the century which briefly won favor in this country as imports. Soon American wicker manufacturers had recognized the trend toward upholstery, and by 1910, cushions filled with horsehair or cotton and covered in cretonne, velour, chintz, linen, canvas, satin, or leather began appearing in showrooms. Wicker of this era relied heavily on padded cushion backs as well as cushioned and innerspring seats. The gradual and almost imperceptible shift in public taste from woven reed and cane seats to upholstered seats with innerspring cushions took a mere decade.

Staining, painting, and upholstery aside, contemporary eclectic decorating trends of the 1980s have bridged the gap into the 1990s. Today's artistic-minded homeowners continue to mix different periods of antique furniture with modern designs. This creative mixing encourages a dialogue between objects. It gives birth to a visual and emotional energy that results in artful interior decoration.

As early as 1917 Walter Dyer had reported in *The Art World* that Americans were beginning to understand the eclectic principle in home furnishing. As he saw it,

wicker furniture, with the appropriate upholsterings, offers an opportunity for color treatments which is impossible with heavier and more sombre materials. . . . One does not need to have a room furnished entirely in wicker. A few pieces contrast pleasantly with more formal furnishings, adding a note of comfort and seldom suggesting discord.

There is a certain challenge in placing eighteenth-, nineteenth-, and twentieth-century art and antiques within a modern context. If it is done with care, the result is a home with fascinating dualities that enhance each other rather than clash. Is it written in stone somewhere that urban and country, traditional and experimental, contemporary and antique elements cannot complement each other? Today the eclectic vision of mixing eras, styles, and materials has been accepted, and the results are surprisingly vibrant.

The world of wicker furniture now influences interior design to a tremendous degree. Victorian and Art Deco wicker can work together when a little imaginative decorating comes into play. The many wicker "reform" movements of the past are now recognized as being reactionary in the extreme. Gustav Stickley's heated turn-of-the-century harangues about "imitation palaces filled with gilt complexes" were an overreaction to ornate Victorian furniture design and architecture; a mere twenty years later Stickley himself was criticized for lacking the foresight to adapt his own designs to take advantage of the machine.

In the 1990s, options will continue to open up in decorating with antique wicker furniture. The stereotypical little girl's wicker bedroom complete with cutesy touches like gingham and organdy fabrics, bows, ruffles, and rainbows belongs in a time capsule.

The Victorian Age, with its uninhibited mingling of competing styles, was really the original eclectic era. Its spirit has now come full circle.

A *dormered sitting room features a Victorian wicker rolled-arm settee, used here to display an antique bisque doll collection. The rocker from the same era has an unusual star and crescent moon motif and both pieces employ star-caned back panels. The green taboret adds a touch of color and mixes well with the French wire accent pieces.*

Well-known West Coast antiques dealers have used this Heywood Brothers and Company Victorian reception chair in an entrance to their Spanish-style home. The piece has its original finish with two additional colors on its wooden beadwork. A French Art Nouveau birdcage at right rests comfortably on a Biedermeier table. The varied colors of the obelisk collection enhance the warm tones of the California adobe.

Having no less than 102 curlicues, a closely woven set-in caned top, and a circular woven bottom shelf, this 1880s square wicker table adds a strong exotic flavor to a California living room. The Italian directoire (circa 1720), rich Sarouk carpet, leather sofa, and stenciled walls combine easily and create an exciting mixture of colors and textures.

Afternoon tea was an essential part of life from Victorian times through the 1920s, and many wicker tea carts were manufactured during this period. Doubling as an occasional table, this 1920s tea wagon has glass drop doors and a removable glass tray. A nineteenth-century shoemaker's box serves as a coffee table between a pair of upholstered Victorian chairs.

∽

Pint-sized comfort is the keynote, as a grouping of wicker children's rockers adds a whimsical touch to a country-style family room. From left to right: a turn-of-the-century rolled-arm design, an 1880s design with star-caned back, and a rare wingback design with a magazine holder on the side of one arm.

∽

This Victorian serpentine rolled-arm rocker with hand-caned back panel and dark finish, circa 1915 willow table, and 1920s Lloyd Loom machine-woven lamp prove that various eras of wicker design not only can coexist but can greatly complement each other.

∽

The texture of the sisal carpet and rich wood tone of the Welsh cupboard accentuate a variety of weaves and designs that are incorporated into this simple turn-of-the-century wicker Morris chair. The influential English architect and designer William Morris's rule was "Have nothing in your house that you do not know to be useful, or believe to be beautiful."

∽

A masculine-looking Lloyd Loom armchair, enhanced by the tricolored fiber and diamond design woven into its back, is the focal point for a gentleman's dressing room. The 1920s wicker piece contrasts nicely with the English Victorian walnut footstool and dresser.

∽

Delicate rose-patterned chintz cushions soften this darkly stained rolled-arm Victorian wicker rocker. The white lace table coverlet has the same effect under the natural-wicker table lamp made in 1912. The dark furniture and oil painting stand out against the light walls and whitewashed floor.

∽

97

 Just outside the master bathroom with its sunken tub, this turn-of-the-century armchair provides a secluded hideaway for sunning.

℘

The curved ornamental latticework walls on this Victorian sun porch serve as a perfect backdrop to accent the open weave of this Mission-style wing-back armchair and turn-of-the-century rolled-arm rocker. The large 1890s wicker planter, flowery pillows, and window sash were added by Hingham, Massachusetts, decorator Carol Ann Dahill to create the mood of indulgent taste of the Victorian era.

℘

Nantucket Harbor is viewed through the windows of this glassed-in summer house porch. While the rolled-arm rocker in the foreground and the armchair to the right were both manufactured around 1890, the armchair is not original, having undergone extensive upholstery work to cover up damaged reeds. The 1920s sofa with its crisp blue-and-white upholstery is most inviting; the Lloyd Loom table in the center of the room was once a side table but has been lowered to coffee-table size to fit the needs of the room.

99

The sunny corner of a Conyer's Farm family room mixes a Victorian highchair with a hand-caned Anglo-Japanesque fanback motif and a 1920s library table. A Raggedy Ann collection and quilts add color and warmth to the white-on-white background.

A lavish Victorian standing crib and rolled-arm lady's rocker help create a light and cheerful mood in a baby's nursery. The Goldilocks and the Three Bears antique painting is a signed watercolor-and-pencil original. The wicker baby scale on the desk is from the 1920s.

At first glance the flamboyantly ornate wicker in this sitting room corner looks more like a lacy cut-out valentine than functional furniture. But don't let the abundance of scrollwork, curlicues, and beadwork fool you; these are sturdy pieces, made by exacting Victorian craftsmen in the 1880s, that show no sign of weakness more than a century later. The Eiffel Tower–base floor lamp is the only piece from another period, dating from around 1915.

∽

This charmingly eclectic mixture of wicker styles from various periods proves that a collection or room setting does not have to center on one particular era. The serpentine Victorian armchair and round table, table lamp from 1915, and upholstered Lloyd Loom chaise longue from the late 1920s complement one another and create an informal corner for reading or conversation.

∽

Brightly colored stripes contrast with stained turn-of-the-century armchairs. Between the chairs, an eighteenth-century tavern table is accented by English blue willow china and a nineteenth-century rooster weathervane that keeps watch over Nantucket Harbor.

A Victorian natural wicker doll buggy is displayed on a built-in dining room buffet. The carriage is extremely rare: constructed in the shape of a shoe, it includes such details as crisscross reed "shoelaces," a black wooden heel, and stenciled "stitching" along the sole. The other toys—a folk art church and a French birdcage with mechanical singing birds—are from the same era.

102

Often a single piece of wicker, if stylish and well placed, can make a dramatic difference in a room. This lavish Victorian sewing basket has beaten the odds by making it through a full century with its original light-blue and gold-leaf factory finish.

A beautiful carved-pine fireplace mantel in this family room is complemented by a white children's rocker from the 1920s and a blue-gray Victorian sewing basket, here used as a plant stand.

In a bedroom dominated by a contemporary black-and-white checkerboard tile fireplace, two children's wicker pieces from different eras create a subtle balance. The rolled arm rocker at left is from the 1890s; the two-tone willow armchair on the right, from the late 1920s. Both pieces seat original rag dolls made by artist Jane Cather of Carmel Valley, California. Other small treasures above the mantel include toys, doll-size furniture, and folk art.

There is something magical about the amber firelight casting a warm glow on natural wicker in this cozy living room. The late-Victorian wicker sewing basket was made by the Heywood Brothers and Wakefield Company. The natural 1890s rolled-arm rocker has contrasting open and tight weaving techniques. The small beaded ottoman from the same era adds a graceful accent to an artful setting.

A *fine collection of art glass lamps creates a dreamy poetic aura for the four-piece set of late 1920s stick wicker in this Berkshire cottage. The sofa, armchair, rocker, and library table have original colored reeds. The Victorian bamboo magazine stand in the background, with its Japanese fan motif, carries out the straight lines of the wicker furniture.*

❧

Cape Cod light casts its golden hues on this white Victorian settee and matching side chair. The crisscross reed grillwork, rolled back and arms, curlicues, and cabriole legs contrast dramatically with the contemporary table and chairs designed by Thomas Moser of Portland, Maine. The kitchen itself was the last project of famed designer Teruo Hara.

❧

Mixing Victorian and 1920s designs is the theme of this bedroom sitting area. The closely woven reed rocker from the 1920s has a diamond design in its fan-shaped backrest and a functional magazine pocket built into one arm. The upholstered Victorian armchair balances the small fancy side table from the 1880s. The collection of turn-of-the-century American pottery on the bookshelf is Van Briggle.

∽

Although the oak-topped serving table dates from the 1920s and the rocker was made around the turn of the century, the overall feeling of this room is definitely Victorian.

∽

THE GREAT OUTDOORS

*T*ODAY MANY PEOPLE STILL CLING TO the misconception that wicker furniture was originally made primarily for the outdoor porch or garden. They overlook the fact that our Victorian ancestors readily accepted wicker music stands, vanities, reception chairs, picture frames, bookcases, étagères, piano chairs, and china cabinets—all obviously designed for indoor use. Of course, this doesn't mean that wicker was never used outdoors. Because of their light weight, armchairs, rockers, and tables were often moved outside on a warm spring day or placed on porches for the entire summer season. If a sudden rain shower should come along, no one was terribly concerned because wicker's durable, water-resistant nature was well publicized by manufacturers.

By the turn of the century the widespread use of home elec-

tricity and central heating resulted in what were called "outdoor rooms." Across the country, spacious family areas and sun parlors were created by glassing in porches. These rooms, warmed by the relatively new hot-air heating systems, offered all the creature comforts while at the same time giving the illusion of being outside and closer to nature.

Wicker, always popular on open porches, had no difficulty making a transition to the outdoor room. The big difference now was that many larger wicker pieces, such as chaise longues, settees, and tables, could be placed in the enclosed porches and used all year. Sometimes referred to as sleeping porches or fresh air parlors, these sunny little rooms were perfect for reading, napping, or casual breakfasts.

Some home floorplans of this era cleverly incorporated the popular glassed-in "piazza" idea and placed it in a more private area. In the August 1904 issue of *The Delineator*, Alice M. Kellogg wrote in her article "New Ideas for Porch Furnishing" that the porch had recently undergone a perceptible change in its relation to the house:

Incorporated as it formerly was with the front entrance to the house, the piazza was decidedly lacking in the element of privacy. The newer architecture increases the advantages of an outdoor sitting place by detaching it from the main entranceway into the house, giving it freedom from interruptions and a needed seclusion.

Many people simply screened in their porches to allow cool breezes to filter through while keeping insects outside. Whether glassed in, screened, or left in their original condition, porches tended to be furnished with wicker to maintain an airy, casual quality and, ideally, relate to the outdoors in feeling.

Until the 1930s it was common practice to bring wicker out of the basement in the late spring and give it a new coat of paint for a bright new look for the summer. The great majority of wicker pieces used outdoors and on open porches were painted. It was practically a summer ritual. During twenty years of restoring antique wicker furniture, we've come across porch rockers with more than a dozen coats of paint globbed on. In many cases, the paint is chipped or has cracked over the years, and fine detail work in the weave has been plastered over with thick coats of paint much like a 1950s stucco "remodeling" job done on a hapless Victorian house.

Sloppy seasonal paint jobs not only muddled the design of a given piece of wicker, they also sealed the porous reed or willow to such a degree that it could not benefit from a summer shower or even a thin covering of morning dew. Yet wicker pieces made from natural materials need moisture if they are to retain their inherent elasticity. The result was often a hopelessly brittle, dried-out, rigid piece of wicker, essentially held together by successive coats of paint.

Many larger Victorian and turn-of-the-century homes also relied on sun rooms and conservatories to give them an outdoor feel and to display their horticultural efforts. Ferns, potted plants, and dried flowers would usually share the spotlight with wicker furniture, jardinieres, ferneries, and metal-lined plant stands. Like the expertly restored example at the Mark Twain House in Hartford, Connecticut, most conservatories had tiled floors, glass-paned walls, small cast-iron fountains, rookeries, and urns. For homes with spacious grounds, gazebos were also tremendously popular outdoor structures. They were often filled with wicker furniture for casual luncheons or lazy summer dreaming.

Aside from being popular in homes around the country, wicker was also considered the ideal furniture for summer cottages, vacation cabins, hotels, mountain resorts, and seaside watering places. Americans who migrated each summer from cities for fresh air and to get back to nature found that wicker invoked a casual atmosphere of relaxation and leisure time. This nineteenth- and early twentieth-century association of wicker with vacation destinations and the great outdoors is still a strong image. When harried urbanites fled hectic city life for their sojourn at the seashore or into the mountains, even their mode of transportation was furnished with wicker. The luxurious cars on most summer excursion train routes were filled with wicker armchairs with thick rolled arms and backs as well as sturdy wicker side tables.

Once travelers arrived at their destinations they found wicker in hotel entrance halls, lobbies, and reading rooms. Outdoors, wicker was again the furniture of choice, filling open-air sleeping porches, expansive wraparound verandas, rolling lawns, gardens, and the banks of tranquil lakes as well as gracing the darling of outdoor architecture, the gazebo.

A perpetual favorite at the seashore, hooded wicker chairs fashioned after the sixteenth-century French *guérite* dotted the beaches, while wicker board-

walk chairs on wheels rolled their way down Atlantic City boardwalks. Sea breezes and wicker seemed to be a marriage made in heaven; from Martha's Vineyard to the California coast, the Jersey shore to the Florida Keys, wicker was there in abundance. Indeed, many wicker designs were eventually named after popular East Coast seaside resorts, including Bar Harbor, Cape Cod, Newport, and Southampton. Interestingly, even the yachts of this era were amply furnished with quality wicker.

From wicker's frequent link to outdoor summer activities in illustrations from magazine advertisements and romantic novels prior to 1920, to modern magazine editors who still insist on clinging to the myth that wicker should be thought of as a summer item, it's not hard to see why some of these woven masterpieces have been unfairly placed in the narrow classification of "outdoor" furniture.

Summertime nostalgia on the lake. This wonderful 1890s wicker rocker has rolled arms, a woven center medallion, scrollwork, curlicues, and Turkish-roll legs above the rockers. The closely woven oak-topped table from the same era employs graceful serpentine edges while the 1920s planter makes use of unusually long Bar Harbor–style skirting (above and far left).

ᔕ

The majestic lines of this late-1880s gazebo (top left and right) located in western New York State on Keuka Lake, one of the Finger lakes, was a stopping point for old steamers. A small round table and two ornate reception chairs from the 1890s are used for intimate picnics in the gazebo.

∽

Midnight champagne for two is set out in the gazebo (left). The pair of turn-of-the-century florist's candelabra are made of reed and sea grass. The 1920s table with its skirted gallery makes a convenient serving piece. The Victorian reception chairs incorporate different designs. The one at right has turned wooden knobs, sea-grass braiding, a pinwheel-woven seat, and scalloped weaving; the other has star-caning, birdcaging with wooden beads, plied-reed knobs, and a set-in cane seat.

∽

Twin Bar Harbor rockers form part of a tranquil
summertime lakeside setting. The small smoking stand
is used here as a candleholder.

Sit back and listen to the waves meet the shore on a sultry day on Long Island Sound. This fabulous Art Deco wicker set has a variety of intricate designs woven over a large sturdy frame. The serving table has a built-in metal ice bucket in the center and divided space around it for cups.

ഗ

After an afternoon of sailing on Keuka Lake in upstate New York, sit back in comfort in these rolled-arm Victorian wicker rockers. The dock-side lemonade is served on a portable tilt-top wicker table from the 1920s.

ഗ

115

The sweeping grounds of
Conyer's Farm in Green-
wich, Connecticut, serve
as a perfect backdrop
for this classic wicker
porch setting.

Reminiscent of the
Gatsby era, this chintz-
upholstered Bar Harbor
suite dates from the 1920s.

116

his black 1920s desk and chair faces a sweeping view of the grounds of a Twin Lakes Berkshire summer home. A 1910 Mission-style settee is in the background.

∽

Mixing various colors of wicker together adds dimension and flair to a New England porch setting. The dazzling Art Deco couch has its original turquoise paint with black and red highlights. The chaise longue, ottoman, and couch, also from the 1920s, are painted a far more subdued white. The pedestal and jardiniere are Weller.

∽

Striking black-painted wicker seating covered in a bold print and dating from a variety of eras dominates the porch in a mountain setting.

Upholstered Bar Harbor armchairs around a 1920s dining table and a porch swing from the same era add satisfying comfort to a Boston area porch. The chairs were originally from the Harvard Square Theater in Cambridge, Massachusetts, installed there in 1926 by the Heywood-Wakefield Company which, at the time, also manufactured institutional furniture.

119

Late-afternoon shadows cast a veiled light on a wicker-
furnished porch in upstate New York. The matching
1920s couch and armchair incorporate several distinct
weaves; their gently sloping arms make them both graceful and comfortable. The small hexagonal-shaped table
has a gallery-edged bottom shelf.

The latticework incorporated into this California gazebo complements the weave of a white wicker dining set from the 1920s. The round table has a golden-oak top and matching straight-back chairs—a perfect setting for a carefree summer meal.

Although both of these ornate reception chairs are Victorian, they are uniquely different: one with tightly woven reed-work and curlicues, the other employing open stick-and-ball work. The turn-of-the-century side table is simple but also unusual with its square top and four-leaf clover bottom shelf. All three pieces look lovely in their lush terrace garden setting.

Tucked away in a lush garden courtyard, a freshly painted white Bar Harbor–style wicker set is ready for another summer of casual outdoor use.

This tranquil shaded setting in Carmel, California,
is the essence of a secret garden retreat. The stone
path leads through a Gothic archway to a comfortable
Victorian wicker rocker.

Poolside comfort is the keynote as this three-piece matching set of Heywood-Wakefield wicker creates a wonderfully languorous patio setting. The original dark-green paint is highlighted with a lighter shade to accentuate the woven diamond pattern and also completely outlines each piece.

Blazing fall color is enjoyed on an autumn day in New England with this turn-of-the-century dining table and four matching chairs. The colorful Majolica and Fiesta Ware compete in dazzling brightness with the hydrangea hedge.

124

This 1920s green uphol-
stered settee and matching
armchair are perfect for
sitting and gazing out
over the wonders of a very
private garden nestled off
one of the rooms at
the Charlotte Inn on
Martha's Vineyard.

Ivy festooned over a lat-
ticework fence, a French
enamel table, and an old
wire birdcage add a defi-
nite French flair to this
northern California coun-
try home. The fanciful
open-weave Victorian
wicker rocker lends
itself nicely to this
casual setting.

Old wicker has always been a popular and easily moved form of garden furniture. Viewed through a French wrought-iron baker's table, these twin Bar Harbor armchairs have been comfortable stand-bys for decades.

❧

This inviting garden setting is actually in an enclosed courtyard in a Monterey, California, adobe. Of different Victorian styles but equally pleasing, the two rockers harmonize amazingly well. A lowered Lloyd Loom table and 1910 fernery add their contributions to the casual mood.

❧

Classical elegance is
added to a Cape Cod
porch by a rolled-arm Victorian settee with circular
star-caned back panels
and a set of ornate
matching armchairs.

ら

127

A *spirit of perennial summer is conveyed on a Potomac, Maryland, deck. A matching pair of Victorian loveseats, a 1920s muffineer, and a Turkish bench —used here as a side table —are tributes to the glories of the good old summertime.*

❦

A *classic 1898 Heywood Brothers and Wakefield Company conversation chair and two-tiered side table from the same period are perched on the deck of a Woods Hole summer house on Cape Cod with a sweeping view of the harbor.*

❦

The contrast of white wicker on green grass makes for a cool setting on a lazy summer afternoon. The Bar Harbor armchair has a matching upholstered ottoman, and the unusual chaise longue has only one arm for easy access. All the pieces in this attractive set employ plied-reed pineapple feet.

✑

The last rays of California sunlight on a January afternoon are reflected on the shell-back design of this Victorian wicker reception chair in a quiet courtyard. The two-tiered square table, circa 1915, has a variety of weaves. The carved stone fountain in the background is Venetian.

✑

129

Wouldn't you like to dock your boat at this Nantucket pier and relax in one of these spectacular Art Deco wicker pieces? The striking tricolor paint job is original. The half-round side table is from the same era.

∽

After a tough tennis match, players can take a well-deserved breather on these inviting 1920s wicker pieces. The matching set includes an armchair, ottoman, and rocker which have been painted a light honey color with a navy-blue accent outlining the diamond patterns.

∽

In a Washington, D.C.–area terrace garden, three styles of Victorian reception chairs are successfully combined with the straight lines of a 1920s dining table. The antique flower-gathering basket, on a spike for easy garden transport, is filled with late summer dahlias.

PHOENIX RISING

*B*Y 1970 A PERCEPTIVE vanguard of collectors, antiques dealers, interior designers, and investors had rediscovered American antique wicker furniture. The style, versatility, comfort, low maintenance, durability, and decorative charm of wicker could no longer be denied. Much like the mythical phoenix, it rose from the ashes of its funeral pyre. After more than two decades of acceptance, we now understand that its dramatic renaissance was born out of a nostalgic longing for style, grace, and quality hand workmanship. These same qualities will continue to play a major role in the ongoing wicker revival of the 1990s.

Today's prospective buyers of antique wicker furniture should first thoroughly educate themselves in the field before starting a collection. Read all the books and magazine articles about wicker that you can find. Visit antiques shops on a regular basis and ask the owners if they have wicker furniture or if they know anyone who does. Attend flea markets, antiques shows, and auctions. Even check garage sales; a great piece of wicker might show up at a tag sale a block from your home. It's up to you to know your wicker. The only way to accomplish this is to expose yourself to a lot of genuine antique wicker, and after a while you'll develop an eye for quality, age, and rarity.

The best source for fine wicker furniture is the antique wicker specialty shop (see Directory). Over the past two decades these shops have been sprouting up across the country and have played a major role in the wicker revival. Their owners not only genuinely love antique wicker but also have accumulated a wealth of information on their specialty. The vast majority of wicker dealers are happy to share their knowledge with anyone seriously interested in the field. One of the best reasons for visiting these shops is the fact that these experts carry a vast selection of quality wicker. Many of them are wicker restoration artists themselves or can direct you to the people who do their repairs (see Directory). Since wicker dealers have a high degree of expertise in spotting top-of-the-line pieces, and get them professionally restored before putting them on the showroom floor, it's easy to see why serious collectors, investors, and decorators flock to these shops.

Whether you are concentrating on buying Victorian wicker with its dazzling array of serpentine curves, scrolls, birdcages, wooden beadwork, hand-caned ''theme'' panels, curlicues, and sunburst designs, or wicker from the turn of the century and the 1920s with its angular styling, latticework, and thick reed braiding, look for quality. The following should be examined carefully before making a purchase:

- Sturdiness of the framework
- Damage to any wickerwork
- General comfort
- Beauty of the design
- Condition of the finish (if natural)
- Damage to the seat (set-in cane or woven reed)
- Quality of the reeds or fiber
- Rarity in today's market
- Age of the piece
- Quality of the paint job (if painted)
- Overall craftsmanship

After doing some basic detective work and determining the current price ranges for wicker furniture offered through specialty shops, antiques shows, auctions, and flea markets, you should have a general idea of price ranges for a given piece. However, the *ultimate* price you pay for antique wicker will be greatly influenced by the condition of the piece, whether it is natural or painted—unpainted examples bring substantially more than their painted counterparts, especially if the finish is excellent—and if the piece carries a highly regarded company label such as Heywood Brothers and Company, Wakefield Rattan Company, or any combination thereof.

For instance, you might find what you think is a bargain at a flea market, say, an armchair with a damaged leg. The problem here is that you'll probably end up taking the piece to a professional who must first remove the wickerwork in order to make the structural repair and then begin the tedious reweaving process. Furthermore, if the piece is in natural condition, the repair specialist will have to spend time matching the existing stain so the restoration effort will blend in with the rest of the piece. These repairs can mount up quickly, and what once seemed like a real find will often end up costing you more than you would have spent on a piece in good condition.

Investing in exceptional antique wicker as a hedge against inflation has been practiced for the past decade, and we think the 1990s will see a great increase in this activity. While the Victorian era produced the most valuable pieces on today's market, there are still tremendous values to invest in from the early 1900s transitional period, the Mission era, and the Art Deco era—provided they were handmade. From the investment point of view, the key words are *quality* (in both design and workmanship), *rarity,* and *natural condition.* Concentrate on matching suites, platform rockers, étagères, music stands, ornate tables, bookcases, dining sets, table and floor lamps, china cabinets, tea carts, buffets, phonograph cabinets, Morris chairs, chaise longues, picture frames, and piano stools. Unlike gold coins or stock certificates, investing in fine wicker means putting your money into a piece of functional art that can be admired and used every day of the year.

From the lofty realm of museum-quality investment pieces we go to the other end of the spectrum—the lamentable imported wicker "reproduction." These horribly botched renditions of classic American wicker designs have failed in every conceivable way except sales. The flimsy monstrosities appeal to those who naively think that "wicker is wicker," and are concerned only with cutting costs and achieving a certain "look." You'll get even less than what you paid for if you buy these cheap impostors. While most of the reproductions are sold in import shops, department stores, discount chains, and even grocery stores, some of them find their way—either by deceit or ignorance on the part of the seller—to flea markets and auctions, where they are represented as being antique wicker.

Again, here's where education and legwork come into play. Try visiting reputable antiques shops, auctions, and shows to see the real thing and then dropping by an Oriental import chain store to examine the reproductions. You will immediately realize that it doesn't take an expert to tell the difference between a fake and the genuine article. In the course of your comparison between old and new wicker, test the weight; the imported reproductions, made with a rattan or bamboo framework, are much lighter than their antique counterparts, which employ hardwood frames. Also keep an eye out for an overabundance of curlicues and poor-quality reed which exhibits a dry, whiskery look.

Lastly, one of the most common telltale signs of a reproduction is the use of a circular woven reed seat. These poorly designed seats are often the first thing to go on a reproduction because they are inadequately attached to weak bamboo or rattan frames. The great majority of antique wicker chairs, rockers, and settees were made with prewoven, set-in cane seats. Invented by Gardner A. Watkins, an employee of Heywood Brothers and Company, in 1867, the "sheet cane" was woven on a steam-powered loom and then attached to the wooden seat frame by means of a triangular-shaped reed, called "spline." Spline was used to secure the cane webbing into a circular groove which had been cut into the framework of the seat by an automatic channeling machine.

Wicker furniture is often considered flimsy by the general public for the simple reason that they are judging it by the sagging, unraveling reproductions they come across. Imported reproductions are the plague of the wicker world. They have caused immeasurable damage to what was once a thriving American industry and what is now a stupendous revival centering around these pre-1930 woven works of art. To our mind there is nothing worse than to go into a lovely period home, a romantic bed-and-breakfast inn, or a fine hotel where the owners have painstakingly restored the interior to the last antique doorknob and spared no expense on beautiful Victorian wood furniture— only to cheapen their efforts by incorporating shoddy wicker reproductions.

The easy maintenance of wicker furniture has long made it popular with the public. While wicker doesn't need to be waxed or polished, here are a few tips on how to keep it in top condition:

- Dusting can be done periodically with the brush attachment of your vacuum cleaner.
- Lightly soiled wicker can be cleaned with an old toothbrush and a solution of warm soapy water.
- If your piece creaks when in use and is made of reed, cane, willow, or rattan, a simple hosing off will assure its elasticity.
- If your piece is made of fiber or Oriental sea grass, wipe it off with a damp cloth.
- All natural wicker was originally coated with a clear shellac at the fac-

tory, and some of these finishes need periodic maintenance. If the finish seems dull, a good-quality linseed oil, gently applied with a soft cloth, is the best remedy; it will allow the reeds to breathe and give the piece a healthier appearance.

We strongly recommend that you avoid painting natural wicker furniture. There is more than enough painted antique wicker on the market to choose from without painting pieces that are still in their original condition. If you have a painted piece of wicker that needs to be repainted, we would recommend taking it to a wicker restoration specialist for the best possible results. However, if you insist on repainting your own wicker, it is essential to first scrape off all loose chips with a brush and then clean the piece thoroughly. When the wicker has been properly cleaned, you can repaint it with a good-grade spray paint in an aerosol can; many companies now offer a wide variety of decorator and custom colors. Or, for a professional-quality job, use a compressor and get a high-grade acrylic enamel and an enamel-reducing compound to thin it out. Remember, several thin coats will result in a better paint job than one heavy one.

The wicker revival did not happen overnight. Some twenty years ago a significant number of people became hypnotized by the lines of these organic free-flowing designs. Soon others fell under their spell—and the rest is history. Today wicker is everywhere, from front porches to museums. Only now are we starting to realize that this handmade furniture is a bona fide American art form.

This ultramodern streamlined breakfast room is off-handedly complemented by a serpentine Victorian wicker armchair manufactured by the Whitney Reed Chair Company of Leominster, Massachusetts. Andy Warhol's image of **The Witch** hangs above it.

137

The rich wood tones of this library are complemented by
the butternut finish of natural wicker pieces. The late-
1890s Heywood Brothers and Wakefield Company settee
and matching armchairs are outlined with wooden
beads. The 1880s whatnot displays the distinct Oriental
flavor that was so dear to the hearts of Victorians.

Although this music room is dominated by a Steinway grand player piano, a handsome Victorian settee creates a balance and breaks the monotony of the heavier wooden furniture. The 1800s wicker highchair adds a whimsical note.

The clean symmetry and crisp white paint job on the rolled-arm Victorian rocker makes it the center of attention in the garden in front of this converted horse stable. The Yorkshire Grey sign is from an English tavern.

139

The original mustard-color factory paint job on a 1915 willow tea cart enables it to blend in nicely with the existing color scheme in an early American Cape Cod cottage dining room.

೨

Afternoon tea is set out on a three-tiered willow tea cart from 1910 at the Thorncroft Inn in Vineyard Haven, Massachusetts. The Martha's Vineyard bed-and-breakfast inn uses many antique wicker pieces throughout the house to authentically re-create both the beauty and comfort of days gone by.

೨

Square- and rounded-back rolled-arm chairs mix successfully in an intimate dining room. The beauty of the weave on the backs on these armchairs is shown off to best advantage when they are placed in the middle of the room rather than against a wall. The antique mahogany and wire birdcage and stand are highlighted in gold leaf.

141

An Art Deco Heywood-Wakefield library table carries out the linear theme created by architects Shope, Reno, and Wharton in a Greenwich, Connecticut, stairwell. The green paint is original and is outlined with a lighter shade along the top of the braid.

∽

Most people might find a bathroom an unusual place for a wicker piano bench and music stand, but these natural honey-colored Victorian pieces are not only functional, they add unexpected richness and style.

∽

The interesting lines in an Art Deco four-tiered plant stand add lightness to a country kitchen. A wooden carousel pig, wire double birdcage, and Pierre Deux fabric create a charming French country ambience.

∾

A definite English mood is felt in this entry hall. The natural Victorian square table with horse-shoe-shaped sides formed by curlicues blends well with the eighteenth-century grandfather clock, nineteenth-century Carolean chair, and rich fabrics.

∾

By adding brightly colored cushions to a rather formal Victorian armchair and rocker set and draping the floor lamp shade with fabric, a playful mood was created in a Cape Cod summer house library.

An unusual 1920s pedestal dining table with a quartet of outer legs and four matching straight-back chairs overlook Nantucket Harbor on a late autumn day.

144

A *1920s wicker breakfast nook with a built-in table and two chairs is featured in an indoor garden room. Being one entire unit makes this rare willow piece highly unusual as well as very desirable to serious collectors.*

Forest green was a favorite color for wicker in Victorian times. In this contemporary bachelor's kitchen the rolled-arm rocker and wood basket add a welcome splash of color against monochromatic whitewashed pine walls and wooden plank flooring.

An 1890s reception chair invites a moment of quiet contemplation. Its fanciful design contrasts with the simple lines of the wooden tea caddy holding a collection of antique teapots. The basket on the floor is a carrying case for transporting one of the pots.

Pastel-colored accents show off the ornate beauty of this high-backed Victorian reception chair. The extra-long skirting is intricately woven and incorporates interesting wooden beadwork, fish-scales, plied-reed pineapple feet, and a variety of uncommon weaves.

An aura of feminine elegance is achieved in this powder room by furnishing it with a late-Victorian wicker side chair and relying on the graceful lace-draped look of wallpaper by Brunschwig & Fils.

Wicker fits in beautifully in this East Coast seaside cottage decorated with classic Americana. The comfortable rolled-arm Victorian wicker armchair, pine mantel, Nantucket basket, and wooden nautical compass combine to create a truly American style.

∽

A Bar Harbor rocker is strategically placed in front of French doors to entice one to sit for a few reflective moments while admiring the beautiful grounds of Conyer's Farm in Greenwich, Connecticut.

∽

A Victorian recamier with rolled arm and back is cozily nestled in a small dormered bedroom. The early doll's highchair with heart-back motif is part of an antique-toy and -game vignette. The white bamboo side table at right has unusual asymmetrical lines.

ꜱ

A leisurely Sunday morning unfolds in this sunny Conyer's Farm sitting room. The Lloyd Loom settee is stained and has painted black-and-red diamond patterns and braiding. The tea cart, circa 1915, has an oak top and bottom shelf and latticework panels.

ꜱ

Gentle winter afternoon light casts a ray of sunshine through the star-caned back panel of this Victorian lady's rocker in a spacious contemporary California living room.

149

DIRECTORY

ANTIQUE WICKER SPECIALTY SHOPS

Alabama

Allen's Antiques
121 Telegraph Rd.
Chickasaw, AL 36611
(205) 452-0717

Arizona

The Seat Weaving Shop
2238 North 24th St.
Phoenix, AZ 85008
(602) 273-6025

California

Arabesque Antiques
417 Trout Gulch Rd.
Aptos, CA 95003
(408) 688-9883

The Hays House of Wicker
8565 Melrose Ave.
Los Angeles, CA 90069
(213) 652-1999

Legacy Antiques
868 Lighthouse Ave.
Monterey, CA 93940
(408) 373-5131

Serendipity
108 F St.
Eureka, CA 95501
(707) 443-8544

Connecticut

Connecticut Antique Wicker
1052 Main St. (rear)
Newington, CT 06111
(203) 666-3729

A Summer Place
37 Boston St., On the Green
Guilford, CT 06437
(203) 453-5153

Florida

Frantiques Antique Wicker
1109½ West Waters Ave.
Tampa, FL 33604
(813) 935-3638

Georgia

Heirloom Wicker
709 Miami Circle
Atlanta, GA 30324
(404) 233-6333

Illinois

The Collected Works
1405 Lake Ave.
Wilmette, IL 60091
(708) 251-6897

Louisiana

The Wicker Gazebo
3137 Magazine St.
New Orleans, LA 70115
(504) 899-1355

Maine

Oxbow Farm Antiques
Rte. 1
Lincolnville Beach, ME 04849
(207) 236-8129

Maryland

Joan M. Cole Wicker
Potomac, MD 20854
(301) 983-1805

Meadows Antiques
Baltimore, MD 21202
(301) 837-5427

Massachusetts

Corner House Antiques
Corner of Main & Old Mill Pond
Rte. 7
Sheffield, MA 01257
(413) 229-6627

The Wicker Lady
925 Webster St.
Needham, MA 02192
(617) 449-1172

The Wicker Porch
335 Wareham Rd. (Rte. 6)
Marion, MA 02738
(508) 748-3606
Mailing address: P.O. Box 47
East Wareham, MA 02538
Residence (508) 748-0962

The Wicker Porch II
13 North Water St.
Nantucket Island, MA 02554
(508) 228-1052

Wicker Unlimited
108 Washington St.
Marblehead, MA 01945
(617) 631-9728

Minnesota

American Classics
4944 Xerxes South
Minneapolis, MN 55410
(612) 926-2509

An Elegant Place
421 Third St.
Excelsior, MN 55331
(612) 474-5752
(612) 475-2058

The Wicker Shop
2190 Marshall Ave.
St. Paul, MN 55104
(612) 647-1598

New Jersey

Dovetail Antiques
White Pine Rd.
RR 2, Box 194
Columbus, NJ 08022
(609) 298-5245

New York

Buckboard Antiques
Box 129-08
Wallkill, NY 12589
(914) 895-3050

Circa 1890
265 East 78th St.
New York, NY 10021
(212) 734-7388

The Gazebo
660 Madison Ave.
New York, NY 10021
(212) 832-7077

Let Bygones Be!
59 Sea Cliff Ave.
Glen Cove, NY 11542
(516) 671-0404

Round Lake Antiques
Rte. 9, Box 358
Round Lake, NY 12151
(518) 899-2394

T & T Wicker
Rte. 20
West Winfield, NY 13491
(315) 822-3367

Ohio

Gibson-Girl Memories
625 Main St. East
Toledo, OH 43605
(419) 691-1551

The Wacky Wicker Workers
Antiques of Chester
7976 Mayfield Rd.
Chesterland, OH 44026
(216) 639-1135

Wickering Heights
415 Superior St.
Rossford, OH 43460
(419) 666-9461

Oregon

Possibilities Antiques
1249 Commerical SE
Salem, OR 97302
(503) 588-2552

Pennsylvania

Applegate Antiques
100 Lincoln Way East
New Oxford, PA 17350
(717) 624-2137

Rhode Island

Benton's Wicker East
775 Hope St.
Providence, RI 02906
Showroom: (401) 831-8016
Warehouse: (401) 728-5607

Texas

The Old Wicker Garden
6929 Snider Plaza
Dallas, TX 75205
(214) 890-0025

Whippoorwill Wicker Works
811 West Ave.
San Antonio, TX 78201
(512) 737-1531

Virginia

Mr. & Mrs. William D. Critzer
773 Oyster Point Rd.
Newport News, VA 23602
(804) 596-8121

The Victorian Revival
7500 Idylwood Rd.
Falls Church, VA 22043
(703) 573-8516

Washington

Rickety Wickery Doc
3690 Half Mile Rd.
Silverdale, WA 98383
(206) 697-1790

Wicker Design Antiques
515 15th East
Seattle, WA 98112
(206) 322-2552

Canada

Susan's Antiques
585 Mt. Pleasant Rd.
Toronto, ON M4S 2M5
(416) 487-9262

WICKER RESTORATION SPECIALISTS

Alabama

Allen's Antiques
121 Telegraph Rd.
Chickasaw, AL 36611
(205) 452-0717

D & H Furnishings
Rte. 6, Box 39
Decatur, AL 35603
(205) 355-0345

Arizona

Garnett Mills
9995 East Marrill Way
Tucson, AZ 85749
(602) 749-9218

The Seat Weaving Shop
2238 North 24th St.
Phoenix, AZ 85008
(602) 273-6025

California

The Hays House of Wicker
8565 Melrose Ave.
Los Angeles, CA 90069
(213) 652-1999

Lew Tut
2615 South El Camino Real
San Mateo, CA 94401
(415) 345-0709

Windsor's Cane & Wicker
Repair
130 East 17th St., Suite G
Costa Mesa, CA 92627
(714) 645-8448

Connecticut

Able to Cane
New Haven, CT
(203) 624-1141

The Wicker Fixer
Connecticut Antique Wicker
1052 Main St. (rear)
Newington, CT 06111
(203) 666-3729

Florida

Frantiques Antique Wicker
1109½ West Waters Ave.
Tampa, FL 33604
(813) 935-3638

Georgia

Heirloom Wicker
709 Miami Circle
Atlanta, GA 30324
(404) 233-6333

Illinois

The Collected Works
1405 Lake Ave.
Wilmette, IL 60091
(708) 251-6897

Indiana

Antique Repair Shoppe
7222 Magoun Ave.
Hammond, IN 46324
(219) 844-7959

Iowa

Beldings Furniture Restoration
2734 Mt. Vernon Rd. SE
Cedar Rapids, IA 52403
(319) 364-3347

Louisiana

The Wicker Gazebo
3137 Magazine St.
New Orleans, LA 70115
(504) 899-1355

Maine

Able to Cane
67 Main St.
P.O. Box 429
Warren, ME 04864
(207) 273-3747

Maryland

Meadows Antiques
Baltimore, MD 21202
(301) 837-5427

The Wicker Lady of Maryland
505 Jumpers Hole Rd.
Severna Park, MD 21146
(301) 544-1428

Massachusetts

The Wicker Porch
335 Wareham Rd. (Rte. 6)
Marion, MA 02738
(508) 748-3606
Mailing address: P.O. Box 47
East Wareham, MA 02538
Residence (508) 748-0962

The Wicker Porch II
13 North Water St.
Nantucket Island, MA 02554
(508) 228-1052

Michigan

Lois's Enterprises
2444 24 Mile Dr.
Rochester, MI 48064
(313) 726-6444
(313) 739-7721

Minnesota

An Elegant Place
421 Third St.
Excelsior, MN 55331
(612) 474-5752
(612) 475-2058

The Wicker Shop
2190 Marshall Ave.
St. Paul, MN 55104
(612) 647-1598

Missouri

The Wicker Fixer
Rte. 1, Box 283-B
Ozark, MO 65721
(417) 485-6148

New Jersey

Dovetail Antiques
White Pine Rd.
RR 2, Box 194
Columbus, NJ 08022
(609) 298-5245

New York

Buckboard Antiques
Box 129-08
Wallkill, NY 12589
(914) 895-3050

Let Bygones Be!
59 Sea Cliff Ave.
Glen Cove, NY 11542
(516) 671-0404

Round Lake Antiques
Rte. 9, Box 358
Round Lake, NY 12151
(518) 899-2394

T & T Wicker
Rte. 20
West Winfield, NY 13491
(315) 822-3367

Ohio

Wacky Wicker Workers
Antiques of Chester
7976 Mayfield Rd.
Chesterland, OH 44026
(216) 639-1135

The Wicker Picker
530 East Philadelphia Ave.
Youngstown, OH 44502
(216) 782-5466

The Wicker Wizard
415 Superior St.
Rossford, OH 43460
(419) 666-9461

Pennsylvania

Carolyn Volk
240 Neely School Rd.
Wexford, PA 15090
(412) 935-2171

Rhode Island

Benton's Wicker East
775 Hope St.
Providence, RI 02906
Showroom: (401) 831-8016
Warehouse: (401) 728-5607

Texas

The Old Wicker Garden
6929 Snider Plaza
Dallas, TX 75205
(214) 890-0025

Whippoorwill Wicker Works
811 West Ave.
San Antonio, TX 78201
(512) 737-1531

Virginia

Mr. & Mrs. William D. Critzer
773 Oyster Point Rd.
Newport News, VA 23602
(804) 596-8121

The Victorian Revival
7500 Idylwood Rd.
Falls Church, VA 22043
(703) 573-8516

Washington

Rickety Wickery Doc
3690 Half Mile Rd.
Silverdale, WA 98383
(206) 697-1790

Wicker Design Antiques
515 15th East
Seattle, WA 98112
(206) 322-2552

Wisconsin

Country Weavers
1014 Harrison St.
Black River Falls, WI 54615
(715) 284-4651

ACKNOWLEDGMENTS

The authors gratefully acknowledge the valuable assistance of the following antiques dealers, without whose generous help this book would not have been possible: Mary Jean McLaughlin of A Summer Place in Guilford, Connecticut; Frank and Diane McNamee of The Wicker Porch in Marion and Nantucket, Massachusetts; Steven and Tamara Mottet of Arabesque Antiques in Aptos, California; Joan M. Cole of Joan M. Cole Wicker in Potomac, Maryland; Charlie Wagner of The Wicker Lady in Needham, Massachusetts; David Robinson and Michael Canadas of Legacy Antiques in Monterey, California; Thomas and Kathleen Tetro of Corner House Antiques in Sheffield, Massachusetts; Michael Matonick of Richard Summerscales USA Inc. in Monterey, California; and John Keller and H. Lewis Scott of Keller & Scott Antiques in Carmel, California.

We would also like to thank the following people, who were kind enough to open their homes to us and cooperated in every conceivable way to make the long photo sessions as comfortable and productive as possible: Katherine Woodward Mellon, Mr. and Mrs. Patrick Donza, Enid Hubbard, Brook and Nicola Johnson, Barbara Sinclair, Mr. and Mrs. Prosser Gifford, Artie Early, Carol Saveria, Dr. and Mrs. James Wechsler, Sandy Garfunkel, Anthony Cahill, Ranne Warner, Margaret Hays, Carol Ann Dahill, Joanne Bell, Fran and Mary McNamee, Scott and Kathleen Toombs, Theodore and Mary Cross, and Joanne Kilsheimer.

Gary and Paula Conover of the Charlotte Inn in Edgartown, Massachusetts, and the kind people at the Thorncroft Inn in Vineyard Haven, Massachusetts, were also extremely cooperative by opening their beautiful inns to be photographed.

Thanks also to our agent, Susan Urstadt, and our editors, Ann Cahn and Sharon Squibb. At Crown Publishers, thanks to Nancy Maynes, Mark McCauslin, and Ken Sansone.

Last, we would like to thank Gary Denys for his superb photographs and creative input.

INDEX